A LITTLE GIANT® BOOK

WEIRD & WACKY FACTS

K.R. Hobbie, Arkady Leokum, Sheryl Lindsell-
Roberts, Robert Obojski, Michael J. Pellowski,
Joseph Rosenbloom, Doug Storer, William Tichy,
and the Diagram Group

STERLING

New York / London
www.sterlingpublishing.com/kids

Library of Congress Cataloging-in-Publication Data Available

10 9 8 7 6 5 4 3 2 1

Published by Sterling Publishing Co., Inc.
387 Park Avenue South, New York, NY 10016
© 2005 by Sterling Publishing Co., Inc.
Material in this book previously appeared in *Bananas Don't Grow on Trees* © 1978
Joseph Rosenbloom; *Baseball's Strangest Moments* © 1988 by Robert Obojski; *The
Curious Book* © 1976 by Sterling Publishing Co., Inc., *Encyclopedia of Amazing
But True Facts* © 1980 by Amazing But True, Inc.; *Funky, Freaky Facts Most
People Don't Know* © 1997 by Diagram Visual Information Limited; *Funny Laws
and Other Zany Stuff* © 1999 by Sheryl Lindsell-Roberts; *The Funny Side of Sports*
© 1996 by Michael Pellowski; *Loony Laws & Silly Statutes* © 1994 by Sheryl
Lindsell-Roberts. *Poisons: Antidotes & Anecdotes* © 1977 by Sterling Publishing
Co., Inc.: *Things You Thought You Knew (But Don't Count on It)* © 2002 by
Sterling Publishing Co., Inc. and *World's Wackiest Lawsuits* © 1992, by K. R.
Hobbie.
Illustrations © by Joyce Behr, Lucy Corvino, Sanford Hoffman, and Myron Miller.
Distributed in Canada by Sterling Publishing
c/o Canadian Manda Group, 165 Dufferin Street
Toronto, Ontario, Canada M6K 3H6
Distributed in the United Kingdom by GMC Distribution Services,
Castle Place, 166 High Street, Lewes, East Sussex, England BN7 1XU
Distributed in Australia by Capricorn Link (Australia) Pty. Ltd.
P.O. Box 704, Windsor, NSW 2756, Australia

Printed in China
All rights reserved

Sterling ISBN-13: 978-1-4027-4987-2
       ISBN-10: 1-4027-4987-2

For information about custom editions, special sales, premium and
corporate purchases, please contact Sterling Special Sales
Department at 800-805-5489 or specialsales@sterlingpub.com.

Contents

Food

During the sixteenth century, Europe was introduced to a new drink made from a small, exotic fruit. The drink had come from Turkey, but before that the fruit had been used for centuries in Africa. African nomads crushed the fruit into balls of fat and used these as their sole ration on long desert journeys.

The drink was said to have almost magical powers. It could allay fatigue and bring renewed strength; it could restore victims from the paralyzing effects of shock or poisoning.

So great were the powers ascribed to this drink that many Europeans believed it was touched by witchcraft. It became known as the "infidel" drink, and European churchmen banned it.

However, in 1592, Pope Clement VIII came to the Vatican. He was a wise and sensible man, and it was he who cleared the reputation of this new beverage by issuing an order that approved the new drink as fit for Christian consumption.

This controversial drink was our everyday coffee . . . the only beverage ever to be officially sanctioned by the Catholic Church.

✳ Drinking tea, if you're a native of Uruguay or Paraguay, can be quite an experience. The tea is called maté, because it is made from the dried leaves of the maté grass. A few dried leaves are put into an empty calabash gourd, and then boiling water is poured in. A tube of silver, called a *bombilla*, which has pinholes at one end, is put into the gourd, and the hot maté is then sipped through the bombilla.

✳ Most of the people who drink tea have no idea of what it takes to produce it. For example, the tender bud and the top two leaves of the plant are called a tea flush. Each one has to be picked by hand. And it takes more than 3,500 tea flushes to make a single pound of processed tea!

❋ Because protein isn't readily available in many parts of Kenya, the natives drink blood. The blood of cattle, that is. They bleed cows and mix the blood in a gourd with milk. The cow is not injured, and the natives get the protein they need.

❋ During the summer of 1857, the Mabie Circus was making a tour through the southern United States when one of the clowns suddenly decided to leave the troupe. The manager called on the ballyhoo man, Pete Conklin, to fill in.

Conklin did pretty well, but when he asked for a raise, the manager said Conklin wasn't that good. So Conklin quit in a huff. But because he was broke, he tagged along with the circus as a lemonade seller.

One hot day, Conklin did such a brisk business that he ran out of lemonade. Rushing into a nearby tent, he picked up a bucket of water, stirred in some tartaric acid, and was in business again. It wasn't until he poured the first glass that he noticed that his new lemonade was pink. He couldn't imagine how the color had changed. But he decided to make the most of it.

"Strawberry lemonade," he shouted. "Try the new strawberry lemonade." People did try it, and today pink lemonade is sold at every circus.

And how did Conklin's lemonade get that color? Well, a performer's red tights had just been soaking in that bucket of water!

※ The national beverage of the Scandinavian countries is *akvavit* (an alcoholic drink made from grain or potatoes and flavored with caraway seeds). It is not to be sipped but taken at one swallow. And an old Scandinavian custom at formal gatherings is to drink as many toasts as there are buttons on the men's dress vests. It's a mighty powerful custom**!**

※ Not everybody in the world drinks the same kind of milk. Milk is obtained by different people from dairy cows, goats, sheep, mares, reindeer, camels, zebras, llamas, yaks, and water buffalo**!**

※ When some English people want to "clean" their blood, they drink "agrimony" tea. The odd thing is that this tea is made from a weed that grows in garbage dumps and junkyards in the British Isles.

✻ Is it possible to build up a tolerance for the poison arsenic by taking increasingly larger doses over a long interval of time? It seems so. The Aztecs claimed to have immunity (but only up to a point). They began to eat arsenic regularly as children. It is said that their skin color was caused by the peculiar interaction between the sun and the arsenic under their skin.

✻ At certain functions in Scotland, the chefs march in bearing trays of a dish called *haggis*. It's a pudding of sheep hearts, livers, and other innards, boiled in the animal's stomach. This national delicacy is so honored in Scotland that the chefs are led by bagpipers, and the whole ceremony is called Piping In the Haggis.

✻ A maid of honor at an important occasion? That seems natural. But *Maids of Honour* is the name given to certain cakes that are served at official affairs in London. They're very rich and contain almond paste, sugar, butter, milk, eggs, and lemon rind.

✳ Helping the poor is done by people of good will all over the world. We see little cans into which we can drop coins, or people collecting money for the poor, or places where we can leave old clothing for them.

But there is a place in Portugal where the poor are helped in a very unusual way. At the Convent of St. Benedict in Braga, there is an iron fence with a tube built into it that faces the public. And the good people of the community come here to drop eggs into the tube for the poor!

✳ A very important family custom in Nigeria is the naming ceremony. Seven days after the birth of a child, family and friends receive a kola nut from the new father. This signifies an invitation to join in the celebration and praise the newborn.

✳ A visit to Salley, South Carolina, wouldn't be complete without attending the Chitlin' Strut. Chitterlings—hog intestines that are boiled or fried—are consumed by the ton at this festival.

✳ If you ever get up the courage to eat an opossum, you might as well prepare it as they do in South Carolina. The opossum is boiled whole, surrounded with baked yellow sweet potatoes and basted with grease in which the 'possum was boiled, then baked until brown. It's called Carolina Opossum and Sweet Potatoes.

✳ A worm called the palolo lives in the coral reefs of the South Pacific. Twice a year, millions of these worms come to the surface to mate. The natives of the islands stop everything and collect huge quantities of the palolos. Then they bake the worms and have a feast!

❋ Anteaters eat ants, as we all know. They extend their long, sticky tongues and that brings in their breakfast, lunch, and dinner. But who eats an anteater? The natives in South Africa do. They salt the meat of the aardvark, as the anteater is also called, smoke it, and store it to be eaten in winter.

❋ Contrary to popular belief, corned beef and cabbage is not commonly eaten in Ireland. It became a popular food among the early Irish immigrants to the United States because corned beef, at five cents a pound, was all that many impoverished Irish families could afford at the time.

❋ On the average dining table there is salt, pepper, sugar, and perhaps ketchup. Not on the table of a Pennsylvania Dutch home or restaurant! They have a tradition of "seven sweets and seven sours" on the table at each meal, and you'll see these sweets and sours in all kinds of jellies and pickles—lined up, and waiting to be eaten.

❋ A modern food store will carry all of these: dates, olives, figs, pears, apricots, grapes, peaches, melons, cherries, apples, onions, turnips, radishes, cucumbers, and eggplant.

Interestingly enough, all these were grown and eaten in the Near East and India over 4,000 years ago!

※ Pretzels were invented by monks in Southern France in 610 CE to look like children's arms folded in prayer.

※ The Belgians, not the French, created French fries. The Belgians call them *pommes frites*, buy them at stands on the street, and carry them away in paper cones.

※ Although it is not certain who first made chop suey, it is thought to have originated in the mining camps in California. It was a sort of potluck dish made from whatever ingredients the cook, who was often Chinese, had available. Whether or not this is how the dish came about, chop suey is unknown in China and is certainly not Chinese.

✳ Hush puppies are a kind of cake originally made in Florida. They got their name this way: When people used to fry fish outdoors, the savory odor attracted hounds, who would whine and bark. So, to quiet the dogs, the cook would take some cornmeal, scald it in milk, pat it into cakes, and cook it in the grease of the frying fish. When done, it was thrown to the dogs and the cook shouted, "Hush, puppies!"

✳ Tomatoes were once called love apples because people thought they inspired love. They were grown for food by Native Americans long before Columbus arrived.

✳ John Montagu, the fourth Earl of Sandwich (1718–1792), is credited with having invented the sandwich. Among the corrupt earl's vices was an addiction to gambling. It is said that in order to avoid interrupting his card games for meals, he would order a servant to bring him a piece of meat between two slices of bread.

❋ Pigeon pie, one of the favorite dishes in Morocco, is really quite a job to prepare. It can take as long as 8 hours, because the filling must be enclosed in as many as 50 paper-thin layers of pastry!

❋ Oranges did not originate in Florida or California. They originated in Asia and first appeared in southern Europe in the Middle

Ages. It was the early Spanish explorers of the sixteenth century who brought oranges to Florida and, later, to California. Every Spanish sailor was required by law to carry 100 orange seeds with him if he was bound for the New World.

✳ Counting calories is very popular among people who want to control their weight. But the average person still has no idea how many calories there are in the various items of food he eats. Did you know, for instance, that these foods—one egg, one head of Iceberg lettuce, two cups of tomato juice, two pats of butter, and three lumps of sugar—each contain the same amount of calories? How many? Seventy-five.

✳ You may drink a cola and enjoy it, but in Africa they chew it! A kola is the seed of an African tree that is rich in caffeine and has a stimulating effect when chewed.

❄ When you buy a can of sardines, you are not getting one particular kind of fish. There is no such creature as a sardine.

Sardine is the name given to several different species of herring when they are caught while young and small and packed in flat cans for human consumption. One example is the European pilchard, a kind of herring whose partially grown offspring were the original sardines. There are also the New England sardine, another variety of young herring, and the California sardine, a young pilchard found in the Pacific Ocean. In England, the young of the Cornish pilchard are used. The Norwegian sardine is a fish called a sprat, or brisling.

The sardine, in short, is any herring the canner chooses to call a sardine.

❄ Everybody loves a fair, and the Great World's Fair held in Chicago in 1893 was a terrific hit. People flocked to see it from all over the world, as it had, among other new

attractions, the first
Ferris wheel.

But it was a good
concessionaire by the
name of Anton
Feuchtwanger who
was to make a lasting
impression of American
life.

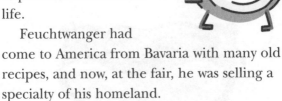

Feuchtwanger had
come to America from Bavaria with many old
recipes, and now, at the fair, he was selling a
specialty of his homeland.

However, because this specialty had to be
served piping hot, it was difficult to handle, so
fairgoers passed it up for more conventional
nourishment.

Feuchtwanger tried everything to get people
to eat his food. He even provided white cotton
gloves to protect the hands of his customers,
but most of them just walked off with the
gloves.

Finally, Feuchtwanger hit on a solution. He would prevent burned fingers by simply putting his specialty between the halves of a long roll.

From then on, Feuchtwanger was a success. The food he served was the spicy sausage known throughout the world today as the American hot dog.

✳ The peanut is not a nut. Most nuts grow on trees. The peanut plant is a legume, a member of the pea family; the peanuts it produces grow underground.

✳ "Fiddlehead" is not an expression of contempt in eastern Canada, it's the name of a green vegetable that is eaten there. The vegetable is actually a frond of the bracken family and is served in the same way as asparagus.

✳ Sea moss makes quite a tasty dish, according to some cooks in New Hampshire. The moss is picked along the ocean beaches. Mixed with milk, salt, and vanilla, it is cooked until thick and called blancmange.

✳ Have you ever tasted *mama liga?* It is a national dish in Romania and everybody loves it.

Mama liga is a boiled cornmeal served as a bread substitute, or with stuffed cabbage or vine leaves, or with poached eggs. Hot or cold, mama liga is quite delicious in melted butter or yogurt. And it can be garnished with salted herring and cottage cheese.

✳ It's not quite a hamburger, but *Chapli kebab* is the Pakistani equivalent. It's a patty of ground lamb, with either green onion or dried pomegranate seed, and salt. In Pakistan you can get this fried meat cake from a street vendor everywhere you go.

Animals

Air-breathing walking catfish, which inhabit freshwater and are native to Africa and south Asia, were first brought into the United States as exotic aquarium novelties. They are believed to have entered American waters accidentally by escaping from a Florida holding pond a few years ago. Now they are entrenched by the millions in the freshwater areas of southeastern Florida, where conservationists report them as officially out of control.

It is easy for walking catfish to live out of water. They are equipped with rudimentary lungs in addition to gills and can survive on land for extended periods of time.

They can also walk considerable distances over moist ground by stumping along on their strong pectoral fins. Generally, they do their traveling on damp or rainy nights. In this way, they are able to move from one freshwater source to another and establish new colonies.

❋ Not all fish have scales. The catfish is one example. Those fish that do have scales are not born with them. The scales sprout later, from under the skin. Fish don't grow more scales as they increase in size, either: Each separate scale just gets larger.

✳ Sharks are fierce hunters. But, unlike most fish, they have no swim bladders (a kind of buoyancy tank) to keep them afloat. To prevent them from sinking, they have to be on the move all the time. A shark can swim up and down and turn quickly but cannot swim backward, unlike most fish.

✳ The electric eel is not really an eel; it is more closely related to the carp and catfish than to eels. One difference is that a true eel breathes in water, while an electric eel cannot. The gills of the electric eel are simply too primitive to obtain oxygen directly from the air.

Contrary to what many people suppose, the electric eel is not unique in its ability to generate electricity. There are many species of fish that can do this. However, the electric eel can generate a greater electric current than any other electric fish. The average electrical discharge is 350 volts, but it can release a charge as high as 600 volts. Fortunately the amperage is low, about 1 ampere, a charge powerful enough to stun a man—but not kill him. This electric discharge is used not only to stun the eel's prey and ward off its enemies but also as a navigational device. It allows the electric eel to make its way safely through the muddy waters in which it often lives. Small electric currents are constantly sent out and reflected by objects in the eel's path, and the animal is thus able to sense the nature of its surroundings. This, of course, is exactly what a sophisticated radar system does. The electric eel not only generates electricity but also operates a true radar system.

❄ Looking like a carved chessman and propelling himself forward in an upright position by means of a fanlike dorsal fin is the six-inch-long sea horse.

Not content with his singular appearance and swimming style, the male sea horse further compounds his strangeness by actually giving birth to his offspring, a procedure considered highly unorthodox for any father, in or out of the water.

A few weeks before the sea horse gives birth, the sea mare has a rendezvous with Papa and carefully deposits her eggs in a kangaroo-like pouch in his abdomen. (The female is pouchless.) Within this protective pouch the eggs are fertilized and incubated.

When his tiny, squirming progeny are finally ready to be hatched, birth pangs seize the sea horse. With delivery near, he fastens himself securely by his strong, prehensile tail to some convenient underwater plant and waits for his quarter-inch babies—the image of Daddy, of course—to leap violently out of his distended brood pouch.

From the time the little sea colts emerge, they can swim and move completely on their own. For a moment, the little ones swarm over the body of the father and then off they go, striking out bravely to meet the hazards of the dangerous, watery world into which they have been so strangely brought forth.

✻ Stonefish are the most venomous fish known to man—and their delivery system is one of a kind, too. They have 13 or 14 *very* sharp spines on their backs, fed from small sacs of venom on either side of the backbone. The sacs are located beneath the skin.

The slightest pressure imaginable causes poison to flow up the spine grooves to the point of contact. If several of these spines manage to puncture the skin, they introduce a most deadly nerve poison into the victim. There is terrible pain, and cases have been reported where death followed in only two hours. More often it is four hours. If the victim is still alive after six hours, his chances for life are good—but not without problems. The excruciating pain may drive him to insanity and, if he survives the pain, his arms and legs may swell to enormous proportions for days or weeks. Finally, nausea may plague the victim for a year or more afterward.

❋ When a whale "blows," it looks as if it is spouting water, but it is really blowing air.

A whale fills its huge lungs with air before diving and can hold its breath for as long as an hour before resurfacing. When the whale comes up to the surface again, it blows out the

air in a great blast through one or two nostrils, called blowholes, on top of its head. When this air, which has become warm and moist in the whale's lungs, meets the colder air of the atmosphere, it condenses into a steamy vapor. The colder the air around the whale, the more visible the vapor when the whale exhales. Much the same thing happens to humans on a cold day, when we can see our breath as we exhale.

Thus, the whale does not spout water. A true mammal, it can no more tolerate water in its breathing system than we can.

❋ There's an old wives' tale well taken to heart by fishermen and their clans about not eating shellfish during a month without an R in its name. Modern biologists tell us it's a pretty good idea, too. Here's why:

During the warm months of the year there's a species of plankton that drifts and floats on the sea like so much flotsam and jetsam. These plankton, called *Gonyaulax catenella*, are strange little creatures about the size of a microbe that by the millions make up the menu of the various shellfish: oysters, scallops, clams, and mollusks. During warmer months the plankton secrete a poison known as saxi-toxin and the shellfish eat both plankton and poison.

The saxitoxin consumed by and concen-trated in the shellfish was at one time intended to replace the cyanide "L-Pill" issued to American agents in World War II. It never really found its way into the cloak-and-dagger arena, though it was used as the poison in the silver dollar carried by U-2 pilot Gary Powers in his flight over the USSR in 1960. Saxitoxin was put into the grooves of a tiny pin hidden in the silver dollar. The pin was to be used in the event of capture. As it turned out the Russians seized the silver dollar, found the concealed pin, and out of curiosity tried out its power on one of their huge guard dogs . . . which died within seconds.

✳ The armor-plated body of the crocodile is lithe and long. (Some have been known to reach a length of 30 feet.) It moves with lightning speed and can kill a man with a lash from its powerful tail.

But it is its mouth that is really frightening. The jaws of a crocodile can snap shut on its prey with a thousand pounds of pressure. A crocodile's teeth are set in its long, tapered head like a row of deadly weapons. Nor do crocodiles have to worry about this natural arsenal failing them, because their 70 teeth endlessly replace themselves.

The huge teeth also intermesh, giving the reptilian mouth the look of a murderous zipper. The croc's charmless appearance is further emphasized by its front choppers, which thrust upward through a marginal groove on the upper lip to jut, tusklike, above its pointed snout.

Though its teeth serve it well, the crocodile *does* have a dental problem. Unlike the alligator, this big saurian does not have a tongue. That means the crocodile has trouble freeing its teeth of debris after devouring its frequent meals. The Nile crocodile solved this grooming problem eons ago, when he formed a strange partnership with the Egyptian plover. This bird keeps the big reptile's teeth clean by feeding on the particles of food left lodged between them.

Apparently the bird's host is content with its "flying toothpick," as the plover is the only living thing that the crocodile has never been known to attack.

�֎ The beautiful fan of feathers you see is not the peacock's tail at all. Those long, lovely display feathers, or train, grow on the lower part of the back, just above the true tail, which consists of 20 short, stiff, plain-colored feathers. When the peacock wishes to show off, the true tail lifts, fans out, and raises and supports the display feathers.

✳ After raising their young, most birds go through a period of molting, shedding their feathers and growing new ones. They lose only a few feathers at a time from each wing, and new feathers quickly grow in to replace those lost.

It is not well known, however, that most waterfowl lose their ability to fly during molting. Swans, geese, ducks, and rails, among others, shed all their flight feathers at once. These birds may be totally incapable of flight for several weeks.

✻ A person with low intelligence is often said to be birdbrained, from the belief that birds have tiny brains. Actually, a bird's brain is large and heavy in proportion to its body weight. Moreover, some birds—crows, for example—are quite intelligent.

✻ The stork doesn't bring babies, as even young people know. But does it have magic powers? Some people in northern Germany think so. They believe that fire never comes to the place where the stork has its brood. So storks are allowed to rest on rooftops of homes everywhere.

✳ The Cass County Quack-Off is held each year in Nebraska, where you can race ducks on the ice. If you don't own one, you can rent a canard for the day. If that event doesn't suit you, you might try the Muzzle-Loaders Rendezvous or the Middle of Nowhere Parade.

✳ Male quetzal birds have beautiful, long tail feathers that were once worn by ancient Mayan chiefs as a symbol of authority. Now the bird is Guatemala's national symbol, and the country's money is named after it.

✳ Old as the dodo and just as strange, but still enjoying life, is Australia's amazing mallee fowl, a bird who can actually tell the temperature.

The mallee, anxious for motherhood but scorning the tedious business of nest sitting, buries her eggs in mounds of earth up to three feet high. As a substitute for her own body heat, the mallee mother-to-be keeps the eggs warm by covering them with decaying organic matter before building the mounds over them. The heat given off by this organic material turns the earthy nest into a fine incubator, and the clever fowl is free to pursue other interests while her brood hatches. Mindful of her maternal duties, however, the mallee returns frequently to test the temperature of the mound and make sure it is kept always at the same comfortable level.

The mallee tests the temperature by means of its long, sensitive tongue, with which it probes the interior of the mound after driving its bill in right up to its eyes. If the bird finds that the mound is growing too hot or too cold, she corrects the temperature variance by one of two methods: either by opening or closing the mound or by raising or lowering its height.

This strange bird can detect temperature so well that even a change of less than two degrees will cause her to take frantic corrective action.

✳ Flamingos get their orange-pink color from their food. They eat shrimps and tiny water plants that contain carotene. Without this food, their feathers would slowly turn a dull gray.

✳ The ostrich can run at speeds of up to 40 miles an hour. On the ostrich farms in Cape Province, South Africa, they hold ostrich races for the benefit of visiting tourists.

✳ Crows make about 300 different sounds to call to one another and to ward off enemies.

Crows live in many parts of the world and, like people, have different languages in different countries.

✳ The kagu is a rather odd bird found on the island of New Caledonia. It runs, but it can't fly. It feeds on worms. And it barks like a dog!

✳ The South African town of Oudtshoorn is known as the ostrich center of the world. It is also where ostrich farming started in the mid-nineteenth century, when the demand for the birds' handsome plumes made for a profitable worldwide business.

Today, the ostriches at Oudtshoorn are raised mostly for their skins, which are used for fine leather goods, and for their small body feathers, which are used to make feather dusters. The ostriches are sheared of these—like sheep—every nine months. Most of these feathers go to France, where tidy housewives still prefer to keep the mahogany bright by means of feather flicking.

✳ It is commonly assumed that one bird leads a flock of birds in flight. The leader is thought to be the oldest, most experienced, or strongest of the birds. This is not the case.

Observe any flock of birds and you will note that the flock periodically breaks formation and reassembles a short distance later. Each time the flock does so, a different bird assumes the position at the head of the flock and becomes the new leader.

✳ Chameleons undergo rapid changes of color, but this has nothing to do with the color of their surroundings.

Cells in the chameleon's skin contain pigments that are involved in these color changes. When the chameleon becomes angry or frightened, nerve impulses sent to the color cells cause the colors to darken. Heat and cold, sunlight and darkness also affect the color of the chameleon.

Thus, temperature, light, and the chameleon's emotions are responsible for its color changes.

✳ Scorpions were the first animals in the world to live on land. They have been around for 440 million years.

✳ The horned toad is misnamed; it is actually a lizard. The remarkable feature of this small desert reptile is that it often squirts a thin stream of blood from the corner of each eye when it feels threatened or otherwise becomes excited. How this happens is not entirely clear, but one theory is that the lizard's excitement brings on high blood pressure, which causes the delicate capillaries (tiny blood vessels) in its eyes to rupture.

✳ With an extraordinary life-span of 20 years, the bat lives longer for its size than any other animal. The secret of the bat's long life may lie in its ability to go quickly into the deep sleep of hibernation. It can, almost at once, slow its heart from 180 beats a minute to a near-death 3, and its respiration from 8 breaths a second to one every 8 *minutes.*

✳ In prehistoric times, there were huge lizards on the earth. They have disappeared—except for one place. On the island of Komodo, and three other small islands of Indonesia, the Komodo monitor lizards are found. They are the world's only living prehistoric lizards—and they often reach ten feet in length!

✲ The boa constrictor does not crush its victims to death. Instead, it quickly throws three or four coils around the animal it has caught and tightens its grip each time its prey exhales. Rather than being crushed to death, the victim soon dies of suffocation.

✲ The common expression "as blind as a bat" is simply not factual.

Bats are nocturnal; that is, they sleep during the day and are active at night. If disturbed and forced to leave their dark caves, they are only briefly inconvenienced. It takes the bat a while to adjust to the glare of daylight, but after that the eyes of bats are as good as those of many other animals.

✲ As hunters, rattlers have several strikes against them. They are unimpressively slow movers on land, with a top speed of three miles per hour. They can, however, swim and climb trees quite well. They are pathetically nearsighted, limited to about 15 feet. Further, they can't hear sounds, but they are extraordinarily sensitive to vibrations coming through the ground. This, in fact, is one of the characteristics that make the rattler a good hunter.

The unique characteristic, however, is the rattler's ability to see heat rays. The snake has a temperature-sensitive eye, located between the light-sensitive eye and the nose, that enables it to distinguish temperature differences of as little as a hundredth of a degree Fahrenheit. To a rattler, a mouse stands out from its surroundings like white against black, though the image is of heat rays rather than light rays. By the combined use of light, heat, and vibration, the rattler successfully stalks its intended victim.

※ Horseshoe crabs are not crabs. Indeed, despite their appearance, they are not even crustaceans. Horseshoe crabs are actually related to arachnids. The nearest relatives of the horseshoe crab are such creatures as the mite, tick, scorpion, and spider.

※ Vampire bats really do exist. They live in Central and South America and feed mainly on the blood of cattle. They bite the skin of their prey with sharp teeth. A special substance in bat's saliva stops the blood from clotting while they lap it up.

※ A hero shrew has the strongest backbone of any animal in proportion to its size. Its backbone protects it from being crushed when it burrows in the ground. It is said a person can stand on a shrew without harming it.

✳ Big ants do have one useful function to humans: For centuries, native South Americans have used the powerful jaws of the insects for suturing wounds. To do this, the torn skin is held tightly together and a big ant is placed on the wound. Instinctively, the ant bites, embedding its sharp mandibles in the flesh. Then the ant's body is cut away, leaving only its sharp pincers to act as a healing "stitch."

❈ What looks like a thick rope may actually be part of the world's longest earthworm, found only in a small corner of Australia where it thrives in the moist, dark soil along the riverbanks of South Gippsland, in the state of Victoria.

These fantastic crawlers often reach the incredible length of 12 feet.

Without organs of sight or hearing, these giants in the earth are harmless and require no food other than decaying vegetation.

❈ The lowly louse was once used to elect the mayors of Hurdenburg, Sweden. In the Middle Ages, the eligible men of the town sat around a table with their heads lowered and their beards spread out before them. A louse was set down in the center of the table, and the owner of the beard into which the louse crawled was made mayor for the following year.

✳ Despite its name, the common house centipede has only 30 legs. Garden centipedes have 21 pairs of legs. However, there are others with well over 100 legs.

Does the millipede have a thousand legs? No. The maximum number of legs is slightly more than 200, and most common millipedes have only 30 to 60 pairs.

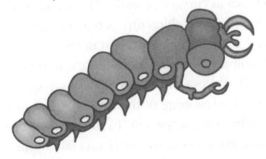

✳ At first sight they look like the worn stones in a giant's graveyard or the ruins of some pagan temple. But they are neither. They are the skyscraper nests of Australian termites. If an army of men were to build a comparable structure, in proportion to their size, it would be as tall as Mount McKinley.

The termitarium, as the mound or nest is called, is a narrow, tomblike wall about 12 feet high.

Because the narrow ends of the walls always point directly north and south, the termites are known as "magnetic ants." The reason for this directional architecture is that an even interior temperature is needed in the mound if the complex termite community is to function well. At noon, when the day is hottest, only the narrow edge of the nest is exposed to the intense rays of the sun. In the cooler mornings and afternoons, the sun's rays fall on the flat east and west walls.

Inside the mound, the temperature is further kept termite-right by a complex air-conditioning system that the insects invented long before man appeared on earth.

Just under the mound's surface, numerous narrow ventilation shafts run from top to bottom. Some of these carry the stale air up to the top level of the mound, where it is rerouted downward through other shafts to be cooled. On its way down, the used air releases its carbon dioxide and picks up fresh oxygen through pinpoint holes in the mound's outer walls.

These walls are very hard. They are made of subsurface soil that blind "bricklayer" termites haul up to each rising level of construction. There the soil is mixed with a secretion from the termites' mouths and used immediately as building material. This quickly dries into a cementlike substance.

The blind bricklayers get no rest until the mound is completed, and termite "policemen" stand by to see that there is no shirking on the job. If a worker falters, it is killed.

✳ If the last 5 of the earthworm's 115 to 200 segments are cut through, it will grow new ones rather quickly. Even if more than this is cut off, the worm will probably grow a new tail, although usually the process of regrowth is delayed and only four or five segments are restored.

However, if the worm is cut in the middle, this is too serious an injury for recovery of *both* halves. The front half may regrow a shortened tail and become a whole (but shorter) worm again. The rear half, however, would not be able to grow a new head. Earthworms have been known to grow new heads after losing up to 15 segments from the front end, but a cut in the middle would remove between 60 and 100—far too many to allow regrowth of the head. Thus the rear half of an earthworm cut in this way will die. (Occasionally it may grow a new tail at the cut end, but—with a tail at both ends—will die of starvation.)

✳ Only the female mosquito eats blood. When it is unable to obtain animal blood, the female, like the male, feeds on plant juices, nectar, and fruit.

✳ Flatworms don't have to go to the trouble of having babies. After mating, they just split into two new worms. Each one is then both a father and mother.

✳ There's the popular notion that the black widow spider seizes her mate with voracious fangs and devours him right after their act of love, which is where the "widow" part of her common name came from. Being anywhere from ten to a hundred times the size of her mate, she surely has the choice to eat or not to eat. The truth of the matter is

that if food is not too scarce and if she feels content enough after the mating she rarely chooses to eat him. More often than not he remains on her web and passes on after a few days, apparently from some sort of accelerated aging process. No matter—instinct makes the male spider eternally cautious. As he approaches her web he inches up slowly to where she is, then he destroys part of the web and isolates her to one small spot. Having done this he tries to touch her, and if she allows he will stroke her. Then he spins a fine web of silk all around her called the "bridal veil." After several hours in the web he finds conditions just right and spends the necessary five minutes or so with her. Then come the fatal moments when she decides whether to eat him or let him be.

✳ The wings of butterflies have no color. All those beautiful colors and designs are produced by thousands of tiny color scales on the surfaces of the wings. If the wings of butterflies are touched when the insects are handled, these scales fall off very easily, revealing a transparent wing underneath.

✳ Two unusual types of creatures have managed to survive in Hong Kong, the crowded island off the coast of China. One is the barking deer, which resembles a dog in size and bark—but has the antlers of a deer. The other is the emperor moth. It's the largest moth in the world, with a wingspan of up to 10½ inches.

✳ If you're in the market for a horse, you might want to visit Virginia when it sponsors the Assateague Pony Swim. A herd of ponies swims to Assateague Island. Then they're driven down Main Street and auctioned off.

❋ Are there any animal fathers who raise their young? In some species of marmosets—small monkeys—the female hands its babies over to the father immediately after birth. Except for suckling, the father does all the work of raising the young ones.

❋ Camels are still the chief form of transportation in India. But what do people do with a camel when they come to town? They "park" them! Camels are lined up neatly on the street, at an angle, side by side, exactly as if they were cars.

❋ Not all dogs bark. The basenji breed of Africa is a barkless dog.

The basenji is a medium-sized dog weighing 20 to 25 pounds. It has a chestnut coat with occasional white spots and a deeply wrinkled forehead that often gives it a somewhat amusing appearance. The basenji is an excellent hunting dog, in part because it is silent during the hunt. While the basenji never barks, it is not mute. It makes noises in its throat, especially when it is happy, but it does not manage a full bark.

One further peculiarity of the basenji is that it washes itself all over like a cat.

✳ The story of Goldilocks is not based on the real facts of bear life.

Male and female bears make loving and devoted couples during the mating season, but afterward the female separates herself from the male and goes off alone to bear her young. She then raises her cubs without the father. If he did come around, he would be driven off by the protective mother. The typical bear family is made up of a mama and a baby (or babies), but no papa.

✳ The elephant does not take water in through its trunk. It drinks with its mouth just as we do, but first it sucks water into its trunk. It then inserts its trunk into its mouth, releases the water, and swallows it.

How do baby elephants nurse? The trunk is pushed aside during suckling and the baby elephant uses its mouth to obtain nourishment, as do all mammals.

✳ With a tail like a beaver's, brown and orange fur, a bill like a duck's, and some inner organs like a reptile's, the warm-blooded platypus, native only to Australia, is the world's oldest and most primitive of mammals.

Although it is a mammal, the platypus lays eggs like a bird. Unlike bird eggs, however, those of this curious mammal have springy shells, tough as leather.

The two-foot-long platypus is a fine swimmer and always lives close to the water. It hides in burrows on land by day and swims all night, hunting down its food. During the night, the platypus eats food equal to half its own weight on a diet that ranges from worms to crayfish.

It also carries a weapon for protection—a sharp spur, equipped with a poison sac—on each hind leg.

At breeding time, the female platypus tunnels far into the earth and makes a warm, tight nest of leaves and tree bark at the end of the passage. Then she seals off the tunnel with more leaves and lays just two eggs.

The platypus babies, at hatching, are only half an inch long and totally blind. They cling to the mother's skin and she feeds them with milk through pores that open up in her chest by means of rubbing.

✳ Some animals retire to underground shelters to pass the winter months when the weather is cold and food is scarce. The life processes are slowed down to the barest minimum to conserve energy and yet sustain life. When the woodchuck hibernates, for example, its body temperature drops drastically and its heart slows down to a pace of only a few beats per minute. Hibernating animals are deeply unconscious.

What about bears? In spite of the commonly held view, bears are not true hibernators. Rather, they sleep during the long winter months. None of their vital functions are significantly reduced. They can easily be awakened from their "hibernation" and will become fully active in a few minutes. Therefore, it would not be a good idea to experiment with a sleeping bear, who might be grouchy if roused from a cozy slumber.

❋ Believed to have originated in the Far East, the Manx is one of the most unusual breeds of domestic cat. It has been bred for centuries on an island off the English coast in the Irish Sea called the Isle of Man. The Manx has two unique characteristics. For one thing, because the rear legs of the Manx are longer than its front legs, the Manx looks a bit like a rabbit when it moves. For another, the Manx is tailless.

✳ Some of the best salmon fishermen in the world are not men at all—but bears. In Alaskan rivers, the brown bears can be seen skillfully catching salmon by swatting them from the water with a swipe of a paw!

✳ When giraffes are shipped to zoos in various countries, one of the greatest problems is posed not by their necks but by their legs. The giraffe's legs break very easily. So if a giraffe slips while on a ship, chances are his legs will double under him and snap.

❋ An unarmed person attacked by a bear is in great danger, but will he be hugged to death? The "crushing embrace" or "deadly hug" of the bear is just a legend.

Bears injure and kill their victims with a mighty wallop of their forepaw. They also use their powerful teeth and their sharp claws. There is not a single instance on record of a person being hugged to death by a bear.

❋ A tiny baby peeking from the safety of its mother's pouch has come to be identified with the kangaroo, but at least 17 other marsupials exist, among them the koala, opossum, wombat, bandicoot, and even a species of mouse.

❋ Australia's red kangaroos can travel 42 feet in one huge leap. Using their powerful hind legs and holding their small front paws against their chests, they can hop at speeds of up to 40 miles per hour over short distances. They hold up their tails for balance.

✳ The bull moose, which is the largest member of the deer family, reaches its greatest size in Alaska. On the Kenai Peninsula there, you can see bull moose that weigh more than 1,400 pounds and have antlers with a six-foot spread!

What is the secret of the Alaskan bull moose's diet? They feed on the tender shoots of willow, aspen and birch, or on underground vegetation found in lakes—yes, they're vegetarians!

✳ Flying squirrels have folds of skin between their front and hind legs. As the legs are extended sideways, each fold of skin is stretched into a flat surface, forming "wings" that enable the squirrel to take long, sailing leaps from one point in a tree to another. Flying squirrels are really gliding, not flying, since their wings do not flap. Bats are the only mammals that actually fly.

❋ Sorry, but all those cartoons that show mice gobbling up cheese as if it were their favorite food, are wrong. Mice do not prefer cheese and often will not touch it if other food is available.

❋ The largest member of the rodent family, the capybara, is about four feet in length and weighs as much as 150 pounds. This animal lives near streams and rivers in Central and South American and swims expertly. Its jaws and teeth are extremely strong, able to cut through a metal bar.

❋ A strange creature called the hyrax can be found in Jordan. It's rather small and resembles a rodent but has hooves and can climb trees. Zoologists are still trying to figure out what it is—they believe it may belong to the same family as the elephant!

❋ All animals need water, but not all animals get their water by drinking. The kangaroo rat, an inhabitant of desert regions in the south-western United States, is able to go long stretches without drinking water, getting its moisture from the plants it eats. Other animals very seldom drink water. Giraffes can go for weeks without drinking. They, too, manage to get enough moisture from the foliage on which they feed. Most sheep and gazelles drink infrequently. A few lizards are able to meet their water needs largely by absorbing it through their pores.

The Human Body

The normal adult human body has 206 bones, but infants have more bones than adults. The underdeveloped skull of a newborn baby has six gaps or "holes" in it, the largest of which is located in the middle of the top of the head. By the age of two, the skull bones have grown sufficiently to close those "soft spots"—thus reducing the number of bones in the skull.

Also, the last five vertebrae at the lower end of a child's backbone gradually join to form a single bony structure, the sacrum.

In addition, the coccyx or tailbone, located below the sacrum at the very end of the backbone, consists of four tiny bones in some people but five in others.

✳ Did you know that you are taller in the morning than at night? This is because you have soft pads (called disks) between the bones of your spine. They expand slightly overnight, making you taller.

✳ Your entire body slows down its growth rate when you get older. Only your ears keep growing.

✳ The human skin consists of four layers. The top, or fourth layer, the stratum corneum, is constantly being shed from the body. No sooner do the cells of this top layer slough off into clothing or into the air than they are replaced by cells from the lower layers beneath. It takes about four weeks for a single cell to rise from the lowest or first layer to the top layer. Our entire skin, therefore, is replaced every 28 days.

✳ You have about 5 million hairs on your body. Many of them are so fine, you can hardly see them. They grow at an average of half an inch per month, but a little faster when the weather is warm.

✳ An adult's brain weighs three pounds, which is equal to the weight of three soccer balls.

✳ Nerve impulses carry messages from your body to your brain at speeds of up to 180 miles per hour—the top speed of a fast car.

✳ When you dive into water, your heartbeat slows down. This is one of your body's survival tricks. It slows down the effect of the lack of oxygen on your body and helps you hold your breath longer.

❄ Your skin helps keep you cool by sweating salty water. On an average day, you sweat about half a pint, but on a very hot day you can lose as many as 6 pints of sweat.

❄ Saying someone is bighearted is considered a compliment. Obviously, the size of the heart doesn't really have anything to do with one's generosity or kindness. The fact is that the heart of the average adult woman weighs about 9 ounces, while that of the average adult male weighs about 10½ ounces.

❄ Your ears tell you if you are standing up, leaning over, or lying down. Special cells in tubes of liquid in your inner ear send messages about your movement to your brain. They help you to know what you are doing.

❄ Are you shrinking yet? If you've reached the age of 40, your body is beginning to shrink. The cartilage in the joints and in the spinal column start to contract, and that causes the body to become about four-tenths of an inch shorter every ten years.

✳ A fetus grows fastest in the three months before it is born. If it continued to grow at that rate, it would be 18 feet, 4 inches tall by the time it was ten years old.

✳ Did you know that when you sneeze, air and tiny particles of mucus are blown out of your nose at a speed of 100 miles per hour?

✳ Did you know that your lungs contain a mesh of very small blood vessels called capillaries? If you laid them out end to end, they would stretch for 1,500 miles.

✳ Because the aorta, the largest artery leading out of the heart, is on the left side of the body, it is easier to hear or to feel the beat of the heart on the left side, just to the left of the breastbone. This is not exactly the position of the heart, however. A small part of the heart is on the left side of the breastbone and a small portion is on the right side. The bulk of the heart is right in the middle of the chest, slightly tilted.

✳ Your brain weighs about three times as much as your heart.

✳ The pupil of the eye only appears to be black; it is actually a hole in the middle of the iris. The pupil looks black because the retina, which lies behind it, is dark in color, and because the amount of light inside the eye is small compared to the amount of light outside.

✳ For the first 40 days of a the growth of a fetus within the womb, it has no fingers or toes—only flippers. The fingers separate around the 50th day, and the toes form a week later.

✳ Did you know that your brain has two halves, called hemispheres? The right one controls the left side of your body, and the left one controls the right side of your body.

✳ Our bodies are more than half water. Men have slightly more water than women.

✳ From all available evidence, no mammal exceeds man in length of life. While stories of extreme old age among humans are often exaggerated (some older persons tend to add a few years), there are many authenticated cases of persons living well past 100. The greatest verified human age has been reported as 122 years.

✳ An average woman weighs about the same as 134 rats. A six-year-old child weighs roughly the same as the air in a bedroom that is 9 x 9 x 8 feet.

✳ Sleepwalkers cannot hear, taste, or smell anything. They only remember what they have done as if they have dreamed about it.

✳ The amount of sugar in the body must be just the right amount, no more and no less— or there is serious trouble. How do we manage this? The brain runs the master controls! If there is too much sugar, it orders the excess amount to be burned up and excreted. If there is too little, it orders the liver to release the exact amount of reserve sugar.

❋ You have about 62,000 miles of blood vessels in your body. Some are as thick as your forefinger, and some as thin as a hair. If they were all stretched out in a line, they would go around the world twice.

❋ Have you ever noticed that you breathe more quickly after you have eaten a big meal? This is because you need more energy to digest the food in your stomach, and breathing more quickly helps supply it.

❋ If you could count all the times your heart beats during your lifetime, and you lived to the age of 70, you would count more than 2.5 billion heartbeats!

❋ When you are asleep your body produces as much heat as a 100-watt lightbulb.

❋ A human has a total of 52 teeth in a lifetime. The first 20 are lost by the age of 13 and are eventually replaced by 32 adult teeth.

❋ Did you know that part of your food-processing system is a long tube called the small intestine, which is coiled up inside you? If you stretched it out, it would be 22 feet long. If you opened up all the tiny wrinkles in it, it would measure 360 square yards.

❋ The human body has about 10 trillion cells. About 3 billion die every day and are replaced by new ones. The cells in your intestines last about 3 days, those in your liver about 18 months. Only the cells in your brain are never replaced.

❄ The back of your eye is called the retina. Although it is quite small, it contains 137 million cells. It has 130 million cells to help you see black and white, and 7 million cells to help you see colors.

❄ If Mama and Papa are proud of how their baby is growing, they're most proud during the summer. Children's growth is most rapid during the summer months, and slowest during the winter.

❄ It's not how fast man travels that can be dangerous to the human body. It's how fast the acceleration, deceleration, and change of direction take place! These forces quickly increase the weight of organs in the body, such as the heart, liver, and kidneys, and put great strain on muscles, veins, and arteries—possibly more than they can endure.

✳ More people in the United States die in January and February than in any other months. The lowest rate of mortality is in the months of July, August, and September. Most of this difference is due to seasonal changes in respiratory diseases, especially influenza and pneumonia.

✳ Did you know that your thumb is a very important part of your body? A bigger part of your brain is used to control it than is used to control your stomach or chest.

✳ A tower of skulls in Yugoslavia was built by a Turkish ruler with the skulls of Serbs killed during an uprising in 1809—as a warning to the Serbs not to try again to overthrow Turkish rule!

Nature

Butterflies can be seen almost everywhere. But on the island of Rhodes there is a place called Petaloudes, or the Valley of the Butterflies. Thousands of bright butterflies are attracted to the scent of the flowers here. In fact, they often fly in legions so thick that they darken the landscape.

Oysters grow on the submerged roots of mangrove trees along Caribbean shores. As many as 50 oysters cling to a single root, and you can pick a whole bucketful in 15 minutes. The oysters are small and sweet. During periods of low tide, you can pick the oysters right from the roots without entering the water.

✳ If you enjoy watching sheep graze in fields, Wales is a good place to do so. There are more than 5 million sheep in Wales.

❋ We associate tulips with the Dutch, but actually the tulip is native to Turkey. The sultans of Turkey were great tulip lovers and had many tulip gardens. In fact, the word *tulip* comes from the Turkish word for turban, *tülbent*.

❋ One of the most curious plants in the world is the rafflesia, which grows in Indonesia.

The rafflesia grows upon shrubs and vines, sending fibrous roots into them. By the time it produces its single flower, all the other external parts have withered away and only the flower is visible. But what a flower it is: A rafflesia bloom can measure 36 inches across!

❋ Have you noticed how those palm trees in hotel lobbies always seem to be exactly the right size? That's because they are a dwarf species of palm tree. Where do they come from? On Lord Howe Island in the South Pacific, people raise these special palm trees for seeds, which are shipped to hotels all over the world.

✻ You probably wouldn't use a lily to defend yourself against enemies—but the early Spanish colonists in Florida did just that. Yuccas are plants of the lily family, and they have stiff, sharp, swordlike leaves. So they were planted around the Spanish settlements in Florida as a barrier against attacks.

✻ In Java and Borneo, in what is known as the Eastern Archipelago, the natives take a very effective dart poison made from the sap of the upas tree and turn it into a super heart poison by adding the venom of scorpions and snakes. The upas is the legendary poison tree of Java. Stories circulated in Europe by world travelers stated that it was so poisonous that just being around it was fatal to all life—animal or vegetable—for miles around, and that its poison was collected by having condemned criminals climb it. (Should they by some very slim chance survive, they were given full pardon.) The truth is that the upas tree (botanically dubbed *Antiaris toxicaria*) does indeed give off a powerful poison, but nothing capable of destroying life for miles around. A speck the size of a droplet of mist is enough to kill a frog, and an arrow prepared according to the Malayan recipe will kill a large animal in half an hour.

※ In the animal kingdom, we're accustomed to the idea of living things destroying one another. But it also seems to take place in the vegetable kingdom.

There is a tall and mighty tree that grows in Costa Rica, called the cenizo tree. When you look at its towering height, you can't imagine anything that can injure it. But sometimes you can see what seem to be ridges in the bark of the tree.

They're not. They are actually the stout vines of a climbing fig plant. And, over time, the vine strangles the cenizo, killing the huge tree!

✳ Living in the trunk of a tree may not be the best choice for a home, but some natives of Kenya do it. There is a tree there called the baobab, with a trunk so huge that old trees are sometimes hollowed out to make homes.

✳ In a churchyard near Oaxaca, Mexico, there is an amazing tree. It is an ahuehuete tree, and its trunk is 160 feet in circumference. How old is it? It is believed to be one of the oldest living things North America!

✳ "The rain in Spain stays mainly in the plain"—as everybody has heard from *My Fair Lady*. But did you ever wonder if that's really true? It isn't. In the north and east of Spain (far from the plain), along the Bay of Biscay and the Atlantic, the rainfall is so heavy that it often comes to 66 inches a year!

✳ Lightning can and does repeatedly strike the same object—be it a lone tree in a field or a lightning rod on the roof of a building. The spire atop the Empire State Building is struck as often as 50 times a year. Are the people in the building at the time hurt in any way by the lightning? No, they are not even aware that the building is being struck.

✳ In a thunderstorm, lightning and thunder happen at the same time. You see the lightning flash first and then hear the thunder because light travels faster than sound.

✳ The tallest clouds are the great towering thunderclouds called cumulonimbus. They can be twice the height of Mount Everest, the tallest mountain in the world, and hold 500,000 tons of water.

✳ Hurricanes were first given names by Clement Wragge, an Australian weatherman. Known as Wet Wragge, he used the names of people he had quarrels with for the worst storms.

✳ The most snow to fall in one storm in the United States fell at Mount Shasta Ski Bowl in California, in February 1959. The storm lasted for seven days, and 189 inches of snow was recorded—enough to bury a small house.

✳ The popular image of a raindrop is that it is either shaped somewhat like a pear with a rounded bottom tapering to a point on top, or that it is perfectly round. Neither is correct.

High-speed photography of raindrops nearing the earth show them to be shaped like mushroom caps. The bottoms of the raindrops are flat and the tops are rounded. The shape is a result of air resistance. As the raindrop falls, the air resistance exerts a force on the raindrop, flattening it. The flattening on the bottom causes the top to bulge outward.

❋ The Kokee area of the island of Kauai in Hawaii is likely to be a bit damp when you visit it. It has an average rainfall of 471.68 inches, and there aren't many—if any—wetter places on earth!

❋ For every drop of rain that falls on Cairo, Egypt, there are 23 times more drops falling in London in Britain. In Guinea, on the west coast of Africa, the capital of Conakry has on average more rain each year than any other capital city in the world. The rainfall is 170 times heavier than in Cairo and 7 times heavier than in London. The least rain falls on the Atacama Desert in Chile. There was no rain at all for 400 years—a record that has yet to be broken.

❄ Because Morocco is in Africa, we expect it to have deserts and a hot climate. But in Chaouen, in northern Morocco, you can actually see snow on trees and rooftops during the summer! The reason is the very high altitude there.

❄ In Switzerland, which is only 227 miles long and 127 miles wide, there are more than a thousand lakes.

❄ If all the bends of the Mississippi were straightened out, the river would be longer than the distance from New York to London. Most maps make the Mississippi look shorter than its 3,710-mile length.

✳ The Mediterranean is the bluest sea in the whole world. This is because the blueness of a sea has to do with its saltiness. Except for the Nile, no large rivers feed freshwater into the Mediterranean. Because it is landlocked and the sun is strong there, the evaporation of the water is very great. That combination of circumstances produces very salty water—which makes it look blue.

✳ One of nature's curiosities is the Reversing Falls at New Brunswick, Canada, where the

St. John River meets St. John Harbor. At low tide the river rushes downstream through a 350-foot gorge and reaches the harbor by a 26-foot descent; at mid-tide the fall is submerged and the water is as calm as a mill pond; and at high tide the inrushing flood forces itself upstream through the gorge in a chaos of boiling eddies and whirlpools.

❄ It's hot inside the earth, and most of us are never aware of it, or simply forget it. But it's hard to do that in certain parts of New Zealand called thermal areas. These are places where the earth's crust is thin. So the energy bottled up below the surface can come breaking through in weird ways.

One such way is in boiling mud pools. The mud pops and plops and sputters about like a porridge pot. Now the curious thing about this is that boiling pools often exist side by side with freshwater streams. So a fisherman can catch a trout in a stream, flip it over his shoulder into a boiling pool, and have it cooked right then and there!

✳ The Dead Sea has no outlet, so the salt that the waters bring into it keeps accumulating, except for what evaporates. How much salt? Well, in a ton of water in the Atlantic Ocean there are about 31 pounds of salt. In a ton of Dead Sea water, there are 187 pounds!

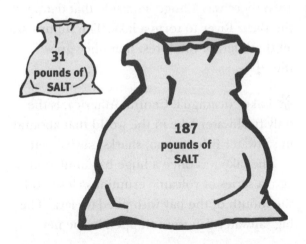

31 pounds of SALT

187 pounds of SALT

❄ Jakobshavn Glacier, in Greenland, travels at the rate of a hundred feet a day. And every five minutes it sends an iceberg into the sea. That's a lot of ice—in fact, 20 million tons of ice every day!

❄ If you go rowing on the Red Lake in Romania, you have to be very careful of the white stumps sticking out of the water.

What are they? The remains of trees! In 1838 there was a huge landslide that dammed the Bicaz River to form a lake. The stumps are all that's left of the forest that once grew there!

❄ Lake Nicaragua, Central America, is the only freshwater lake in the world that abounds in saltwater fish: tarpon, sharks, sawfish, etc.

The lake was once a huge bay until, eons ago, a series of volcanic eruptions closed off the mouth of the bay with piled-up lava. The big saltwater fish were trapped in the new "lake" and, as the water lost its salt through evaporation and became fresh, the sharks, sawfish, and others adapted to this change in their watery world.

✳ Until recent years, this natural wonder of the world was almost unknown outside of Asia Minor: It is the "frozen waterfall" of Pamukkale and is located at Hierapolis, in a remote region of Turkey.

Although it is found in a year-round mild climate, this icy-looking cataract is in no danger of melting. It is a petrified waterfall, formed entirely of limestone, and its Turkish name means "cotton castle."

This marvel of nature is the eons-old result of natural hot springs that gush from the earth less than a mile above the falls. The water from these springs is filled with calcium carbonate, which cools and hardens into chalky white limestone. It flows through numerous channels down to the cliffs of Pamukkale, where it trickles over the rim to form stalactites that hang like huge icicles on a frozen cascade.

Limestone terraces are also built up at Pamukkale, and on these the action of the water dripping endlessly down from above has scooped out shallow pools. As these pools fill and overflow, their water drips down to form new stalactites, producing waterfall upon waterfall.

❋ In 1935, Jimmy Angel, an American aviator, was exploring Venezuela by air when he saw something remarkable. It was a very, very high waterfall. Today, it's called Angel Falls, and it's the largest waterfall in the world—more than 15 times higher than Niagara Falls.

✳ "Russia's salt cellar" is a popular name for Lake Baskunchak in the former Soviet Union. It's a saltwater lake that is continually fed by many salt springs. How much salt is in the lake? Scientists say there's enough salt there to meet the whole world's needs for more than a thousand years!

✳ About three-quarters of all the fresh water in the world lies frozen in the Arctic and Antarctic ice caps. If the ice caps melted, the sea levels would rise by 200 feet and New York, London, and Paris would be underwater.

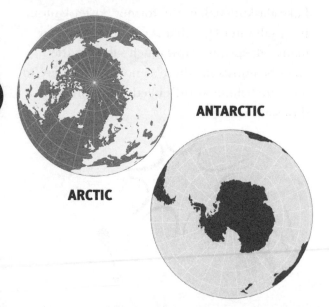

ANTARCTIC

ARCTIC

✳ Strange caves of all sorts attract tourists everywhere, and probably no caves anywhere can match the sight that is provided visitors on the North Island of New Zealand.

That's where the glowworm caves are located, in Waitomo. There are silent, still waters in the caves, and hanging down from the cave roof are millions of glowworms. The worms emit a glutinous thread that glows in the dark, and the millions of threads form a glowing canopy that is startling and beautiful.

To the glowworms, of course, it's all a matter of getting something to eat. The threads trap insects that are attracted to their light. When one of them is caught, the glow-worms gobble up the line with the prey! Tourists keep going way up into the mountains to look at them—but they really have no idea what they're actually looking at!

✳ In the Carpathian Mountains in Romania, there are a group of strangely shaped rocks called the Babele, or "old woman," rocks. They are rounded, thinner at the center, with flat tops, and stand overlooking the valley.

Some experts believe the rocks were eroded into this peculiar shape, possibly by glaciers. Other experts think they were ancient religious sculptures. And the rocks just sit there like "old women," revealing nothing!

✳ The Giant's Causeway in Northern Ireland was, according to folklore, built by an Irish giant named Finn McCool, in order to cross over to Scotland to fight a rival Scottish giant. Geologists believe, however, that the odd formation is a result of molten lava going through a process of rapid cooling, which caused the lava to crack into these strange shapes.

✳ If you consider their total height, from top to bottom, the highest mountains in the world are the islands of Hawaii. The eight islands are actually mountaintops. The mountains rise 18,000 feet from the ocean floor to the water's surface, and two of them, Mauna Loa and Mauna Kea, rise almost another 14,000 feet above the water!

✳ The Kamchatka Peninsula, at the southeastern tip of Russia, is certainly a "lively" place. It has 20 geysers spurting steam and water, and more than 60 active volcanoes!

❋ A volcano is potentially dangerous because it might erupt. But on the Italian island of Stromboli, there is a volcano that nobody seems to fear—not even the birds. It is an active volcano that rumbles away continuously on the inside—yet flocks of birds have made their home on the 3,000-foot cone!

❋ Nobody likes erupting volcanoes, but the Italians have had to put up with them a really long time. In fact, records of eruptions go back farther in Italy than in any other country. Maybe that's why the words volcano and lava are both Italian. There are still three active volcanoes in Italy: Stromboli, Etna, and Vesuvius.

❋ A hill near Abergavenny in Wales is called Skirrid Fawr, or Holy Mountain. That's because there is a notch in the mountain that the local people believe was caused by an earthquake that shook the world at the Crucifixion.

❋ Many people are fascinated by volcanoes. They love to climb up to the top and peer down into the crater—even when fumes are rising from it.

If that's your idea of a fun trip, Costa Rica is a good place to visit. Costa Rica measures only 288 miles at its greatest length and 170 miles at its widest point, but there are volcanoes all over, and many of them erupt frequently.

❋ Nicolaus Copernicus (1473–1543), the
great Polish scientist who founded modern

astronomy, is commonly thought to have been the first to argue that the sun is the center of our planetary system and that the planets, including the earth, revolve around the sun. Actually, it was Aristarchus of Samos who, in the third century BCE, first developed a theory in which the sun, not the earth, held the central position in the solar system.

However, Aristarchus' analysis of the universe was not accepted by his fellow Greeks. After all, didn't their eyes show them what happened in the heavens? The sun rose in the east and set in the west, and the moon and stars turned in the sky. Everything seemed to move but the earth. Therefore, mankind continued to consider the earth to be the center of the universe, the planet around which everything in the heavens revolved. Not until Copernicus was this notion, despite initial resistance, finally abandoned.

✳ If you know where to look in the sky, you will be able to see Venus with the naked eye in the daytime for several weeks each year. Incidentally, once in about every eight years, Venus at night is about twelve times as bright as Sirius, the brightest star in the Northern Hemisphere.

✳ If you ask most people, they will say the earth is perfectly round, a sphere. In fact, it is almost a sphere, but not quite. As a result of its rapid rotation, the earth bulges slightly at the equator and is somewhat flattened at the poles.

✳ People are incorrect in saying that the moon shines. The moon, having no light of its own, does not shine but reflects the light of the sun.

✳ Every schoolchild knows that the earth travels around the sun. The earth circles the sun at a rate of 66,500 miles per hour and makes a complete orbit every year. What many people do not know is that the sun does not stand still but is also speeding through space.

The entire solar system is revolving around the hub of our local galaxy, the Milky Way, at a tremendous rate of speed. The Milky Way, in turn, is moving even faster around the core of a cluster of galaxies. Finally, the cluster of galaxies is also moving at great speed away from other galaxy clusters.

Does anything in our universe stand still? Scientists say no, nothing does.

✳ The footprint left by astronauts walking on the moon will still be there in a million years. There is no wind, rain, or water on the moon to wash or blow the footprints away.

✳ It is a common but mistaken belief that it is cold in winter because that is when the sun is farthest from the earth. As a matter of fact, during winter the sun is closer to the earth than during any other season—about 3 million miles nearer the earth than in the middle of summer.

The tilt of the earth's axis, not the varying distance of the sun from the earth, determines the change of seasons. When this tilt (slightly more than 23°) is toward the sun, as occurs in summer, the rays of the sun strike the earth more directly (and thus bring more warmth) than when the earth is inclined away from the sun, as happens in winter. (This is so only in the Northern Hemisphere; in the Southern Hemisphere the reverse is true.)

There would be no seasons as we know them if the earth's axis were vertical and not tilted. Constant summer would exist in regions near the equator, and it would always be winter in areas near the poles.

✳ The "midnight sun" creates really unusual conditions in lands that lie north of the Arctic Circle. In northern Finland, for example, in midsummer, there is constant daylight 24 hours a day—for 73 consecutive days!

✳ Any two places on opposite sides of the earth, situated so that a straight line from one to the other passes through the middle of the earth, are called the antipodes of each other.

Many people believe that China is the antipode of the United States. Thus, if a deep enough hole were dug in the United States and passed through the midpoint of the earth, the hole would come up somewhere in China. This is simply not the case. Both China and the United States are, in fact, in the Northern Hemisphere. The true antipode of the United States is an area of the Indian Ocean west of Australia and east of South Africa.

✳ How many times can you hear an echo? It depends on where you make the sound. In Killarney, Ireland, there is a cave called the Eagle's Nest. Folks will tell you that if you sound a bugle note there, you'll hear it repeated at least a hundred times!

✳ Stones can't move by themselves, but the natives of a town called Reynoldston, in Wales, think otherwise. There is a huge prehistoric pillar there called Arthur's Stone. They say that at night it goes down to the sea to quench its thirst.

❄ Carat for carat, the ruby is more valuable than the diamond.

❄ Mirages are popularly associated with conditions of extreme heat. The ever-receding puddle on the sizzling highway surface, the unreachable oasis in the desert, these are what come to mind when one thinks of a mirage. Mirages are actually as common under conditions of cold as they are under conditions of heat. Mirages associated with the Arctic are, in fact, larger and more enduring than those associated with the desert.

Arctic mirages differ from their desert counterparts in that they reflect something that actually exists, although not in the place it is located. Whereas the traveler in the desert may see a lake that doesn't exist anywhere, the traveler in the Arctic may see a land that exists—but not in the place he sees it.

Whether an image has a real or imaginary origin, all mirages can be photographed. The lens of the camera reacts to any mirage as does the human eye.

✳ You see a rainbow when the sun, shining on drops of water, is broken up into seven main colors. On the ground, you only see half a rainbow. In a plane, you see the whole circle of a rainbow.

✳ It gets mighty cold in Oymyakon, a town in eastern Siberia. A temperature of –90.4°F. has been recorded there!

✳ What grows in the interior of Greenland? Nothing. What lives there? Nothing. It is just one immense mass of ice, often several thousand feet thick. There's no other place like it on earth.

✳ Diamond is the hardest known natural substance in the world. It can scratch every other material. The only thing that will scratch a diamond is something called Borazon. It is made up of boron and nitrogen.

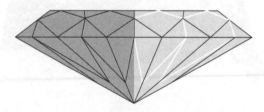

❋ If you measure a day as lasting from sunrise to sunset, there is a time of year in Spitzbergen, Norway, when a "day" lasts three and a half months! The town is so close to the North Pole that the sun shines continuously all summer.

❋ If you stand on a scale at the equator, you will weigh less than at the North Pole. This is because the equator is farther from the earth's center, and the pull of gravity is less there.

❋ Everyone can see mist rising from boiling water but, strictly speaking, that is not steam. Steam is not only invisible, it is not even wet! It ceases to be steam and becomes a visible mist when water droplets are formed by a drop in temperature.

❋ The Danish island of Mano, which is off the mainland, Jutland, is reached by its inhabitants in an unusual way: They drive to it on the bottom of the sea.

During ebb tide, the sea between the island and the mainland becomes a road. There is a track marked by dead trees, and automobiles and carts can go back and forth on this road. But that's only during six hours a day. When high tide returns, the road is covered by five feet of water!

Customs

A gentleman raises his hat when being introduced to a lady and even takes off his hat in an elevator when a woman is present. What is he indicating by that gesture? Respect.

But it all began in primitive times, when captives would be stripped of everything they wore—to prove their subjugation! So taking off some clothing in the presence of others was an indication of inferiority.

It is believed that this custom went through many stages of development, and eventually it got down to the simple act in which men uncovered their heads—to show their respect.

By the way, in Asian countries, the custom is to bare the feet instead of the head. Japanese will remove a slipper when they wish to salute someone ceremoniously.

❋ When you shake hands with someone, you are performing a symbolic act that goes back thousands of years!

Of course, the ancient symbolic meaning has long been forgotten and we all shake hands today without giving the act much thought. But here's what it meant to primitive man:

When a man met someone with whom he didn't want to fight, and with whom he might want to establish a good relationship, he dropped his weapon to the ground. Then he held out his right hand—the weapon hand—as a symbol of friendliness. And shaking hands is still a symbol of friendliness today!

❉ NO TIPPING is a sign we are sometimes glad to see in restaurants or hotels. On the island of Tahiti, tipping is considered patronizing in its most obnoxious sense—and accepting a tip a form of begging—which is why natives refuse to receive tips for their services.

Jon Einarsson

Stefan Jonsson

Helga Jonsdottir

Mrs. Jonsdottir

✳ In general, there are no family surnames in Iceland. The country uses a patriarchal naming system, which means that children's surnames are formed from the Christian name of their father with the addition of *-son* for boys and *-dottir* for girls. Suppose that Jon Einarsson has a son named Stefan and daughter named Helga. Stefan becomes Stefan

Jonsson and Helga becomes Helga Jonsdottir. When Miss Jonsdottir marries she does not take her husband's surname, but is styled Mrs. Jonsdottir. While this is not confusing to Icelandic families, it does cause wonder when Icelanders travel abroad and all members of the family register at a hotel under different surnames.

❋ What is so special about the fourth finger of the left hand? Why does that finger get to wear the wedding ring?

In ancient times according to some experts, the right hand was the symbol of power and authority, the left hand of subjugation. That would explain the ring being placed on the left hand—a token of subordination to the other party.

But why the fourth finger of the left hand? The ancient Greeks had a superstition that a certain vein passed directly from this finger to the heart, which may have started the custom.

But there really may be a simpler reason: It is the least used of all the fingers—so it's not inconvenient to wear an ornament on it.

❋ The number of accidents involving the custom of bowing is growing rapidly in Japan. At railways and airports many people have been knocked down escalators, nudged in front of trains, and trapped in revolving doors. Authorities are planning to install "greeting zones" in potentially hazardous areas.

❋ If you've ever thrown rice at a newly-married couple, you might not have known that you were observing an ancient way of wishing that they have many children. Rice was a symbol of fertility among early peoples and they used it in marriage rites.

❋ The wedding gown is something that most brides are fussy about. But in Scotland, the bride may have problems deciding how she looks in it. In that country, it's considered bad luck to try on the bridal gown before the wedding day.

✳ Everybody loves the bride, but even she has to protect herself at times. And oddly enough, when the bride throws the bouquet after the wedding—symbolically she is protecting herself.

There was an old custom, going back to the fourteenth century in France, of scrambling for the bride's garter. It was considered a lucky thing to get her garter, and everyone rushed for it at the end of the ceremony.

This didn't exactly make it easy for the bride, who would often get hurt in the scuffle. So in time the custom changed to giving away the stocking. And "stocking-throwing" became the bridal custom.

But it wasn't too convenient for the bride to remove her stocking and throw it to her friends. So one bride had the bright idea of throwing the bouquet. The idea caught on— and it's still the custom today!

❋ We call a newly married man a "bride-groom." This goes back to an old custom among many peoples.

On the wedding day, to show his love, the man waited at table on his bride. The word *groom* meant a person who served others. So the "bridegroom" was the man who served the bride!

✳ In Truro, Mississippi, before a man gets married he must "prove himself worthy" by hunting and killing either six blackbirds or three crows.

✳ When people go through all the rituals and ceremony concerned with marriage, they do what is "expected." For example, it is expected that an engagement ring will have a diamond.

Why the diamond? Of course it's a beautiful gem. But the diamond was considered the right stone for the engagement ring in Italy as far back as the Middle Ages! It was known as *pietra della riconciliazione*—because it was supposed to have the power to maintain harmony between husband and wife.

But there is a superstitious tradition that gives another reason for using the diamond in engagement rings. According to this belief, the sparkle of the diamond is supposed to have originated in the fires of love—so only a diamond can hold the promise of enduring love and happiness for an engaged couple.

❋ What would you do with a whale's tooth? In the Fiji Islands, a whale's tooth is very desirable. It is called a *tabua*, and it is presented to distinguished guests as an honor. In a marriage ceremony, the bride and bridegroom exchange whale's teeth. You can't even take a whale's tooth out of Fiji without government permission!

❋ You don't see a man buying his wife when you go to a wedding. But the strange thing is— that's what the word *wedding* is all about!

In the old days, men purchased their brides from her parents. The "wed" was the money, horses, or cattle the groom gave as security that he would purchase the bride from the father. And from this "wed" developed the idea of a wedding!

❊ Giving gifts to the bride is a loving custom people enjoy. In Japan, the bridegroom sends magnificent gifts to the bride—but she doesn't keep them. She gives them to her parents to show her appreciation for their kindness to her.

✳ Everybody wishes the bride and groom a happy honeymoon today. But the idea of the honeymoon actually goes back to the time when it was customary for the newlyweds to run away after the wedding. The bride's kinsmen would go looking for the young woman to capture her and take her back. The husband hid with his bride until the relatives got tired of searching for her—and that's how the honeymoon got its start!

✳ If you think mothers-in-law are unpopular today, imagine how a mother-in-law felt who lived among the Lhopa tribe in Tibet years ago.

It used to be the custom there to eat the bride's mother at the wedding feast! But then, cannibalism was always a painful custom.

There are many countries where parents arrange the marriages of their children. And this is usually done when they reach a certain age and are ready for it.

But there is also the custom of infant betrothal, in which marriages are arranged—and sometimes actually performed—when the girl and boy are mere infants!

In New Caledonia, for example, a girl is betrothed as soon as she is born. In the Fiji Islands, children are married by their parents when they are three or four years old. It's only a ceremony, but it's a binding ceremony. When the children grow up, they are man and wife.

And among certain Eskimo tribes, a young man, or his father, can ask for a girl as soon as the girl is born. If the father of the child accepts the offer of marriage, a promise is given. It as binding as a marriage ceremony. At the proper age, the girl is delivered and the wedding takes place. It sometimes may be the first time she has seen her husband.

❋ Nobody really knows when or where the idea of having wedding rings began. But the first records we have of wedding rings being used in marriage vows occur in ancient Egyptian literature.

Why a ring? In hieroglyphics, the circle represents eternity. So a ring was a symbol of the marriage tie, which is supposed to be binding throughout eternity.

❋ Holding the hands together, palm to palm, while praying, seems perfectly natural to us. Children are taught this attitude of prayer today—and the early Greeks prayed in exactly the same way.

The symbol of the hand found its way into religion thousands of years ago. And that was probably because it signified power. At one time, a subordinate person had to present his hands, joined palm to palm, when expressing obedience to a superior. In religious prayer, the joining of the hands is still a symbol of that.

✳ There are 365 churches in and around the city of Cholula, Mexico. Why 365? One for each day of the year, of course.

✳ At many funerals, candles are set up around the body. This is a relic of an old superstition. People believed evil spirits would enter the dead person, so fires were built around the corpse to keep them away.

✻ The small Greek island of Mykonos has hundreds of churches on it. Whenever a seafarer from the island would go out to sea and have some experience where he escaped death, he would build a church in gratitude.

✻ On Midsummer Eve, in Sweden, girls place seven different flowers under their pillows. This is supposed to make them dream of the man they will marry.

✳ In certain parts of Germany, you'll be eating carp for luck on New Year's Eve. And if you want to be sure you'll have plenty of money during the next year, you should also slip a few of the carp's scales into your pocket or purse!

✳ Men, women, and children on roller skates are a sight to be seen on certain streets in Caracas, Venezuela. It's a custom there for people to roller-skate early in the morning during the nine days of Christmas masses.

❋ Easter customs often have to do with eggs. In northwestern Germany, they have "egg duels," which are called *Eier-Spacken.* Two men face each other, holding hard-boiled eggs by the round ends. The idea is to stab the other person's egg with the pointed end of your egg. The winner: the one who cracked the most eggs. The prize: all the cracked eggs!

❋ The Day of the Dead is a festival held in Mexico each year. It celebrates those who have died, and people have parties around graves, eating chocolates and candy in the shape of skeletons and coffins. In Mexican Indian folk- lore, the dead return to life on this day.

❋ You're walking down a street in Paris and a priest is walking in front of you. A young boy comes along, hesitates, then passes the priest on the street. But then he immediately touches an iron fence. It seems the young street wanderers of Paris believe it's unlucky to pass a priest—but if you touch a piece of iron at once, you break the bad luck!

✳ There is a living goddess enshrined in Kathmandu, Nepal. Housed in a temple next to the old Royal Palace in the heart of the city, she is a symbol of purity, chosen at an early age from a group of young girls by Hindu priests and forced to live alone until she reaches puberty. Another living goddess is then chosen by the priests, while the previous goddess is sent back to her village with a large dowry. As the ex-goddess is considered bad luck, no one will marry her despite her wealth.

During her reign as living goddess she is allowed to leave her quarters only once a year, at which time she is carried about in a religious ceremony. However, she can often be seen at her window inside the temple courtyard.

✳ Lazybones have no fun on Lazybones Day in Amsterdam. At four o'clock in the morning, young people start making a racket by beating on pots and pans, ringing doorbells, and whistling. They march through the town, and any boy or girl who refuses to get up and join in is branded a *luilak* or "lazybones" for the whole year to come!

❋ If it's New Year's Eve, and you're in Scotland, chances are you'll be having visitors. That is, if you're not out visiting, too!

The old custom of open-house is still practiced by many folks in Scotland at New Year. It goes back to a superstition that the person who is the first to visit a family in the New Year will have a lucky and prosperous year.

So when the clock strikes twelve, the people rush out and try to be "first foot." It makes for a rather lively celebration, because each visitor carries boxes of cakes and glasses of spiced ale as he makes the rounds, and at each house he shares a bit of cake and a sip of ale with the host!

✳ Qu Yuan drowned himself more than 2,000 years ago, but the Chinese in Hong Kong still have a festival in his honor every year. The Dragon Boat Festival takes place in May or

June. Boats with dragon heads on their bows go into the water, and rice cakes are tossed into the water in memory of this man. He was a statesman who drowned himself because the emperor had refused to reform the corrupt imperial court.

✳ To begin the Feast of St. John the Baptist, thousands of Puerto Rican families spend the night of June 23rd in front of open bonfires on the beach. At dawn on June 24th, they wade into the water. This reenactment of the baptism of Jesus, they believe, will assure them good health in the coming year.

✳ Christmas is a time when children expect nice gifts. But in some countries, they have a tradition that doesn't always work that way.

Shortly before Christmas is St. Nicholas Day, which introduces the festive season. In Austria, St. Nicholas gives small gifts to "good" children. But what about "bad" children? Well, devils and other monsters, called *Krampusses*, go about threatening and frightening them.

The reaction to this custom varies. Some parents say the youngsters enjoy it, knowing it's all a joke. Psychologists are actually trying to put an end to this practice, saying it terrifies the children. And the "bad" children?—they hate it!

✳ In Florence, Italy, Ascension Day is a spring holiday celebrated with a song—the song of the cricket. The people of Florence stage a Cricket Festival, and sell hundreds of cages with crickets in them. What better symbol of spring, they say, than the chirping of a cricket?

✳ The feast of Narayan in Nepal is celebrated at the giant statue of Vishnu. The statue, carved out of gray stone and showing Vishnu reposing on a tangle of serpents, is covered with flowers, holy oil, and red and yellow powder during the ceremony. The king of

Nepal is forbidden to visit the statue—Hindus believe that the King is a reincarnation of Vishnu and would die if he were to see the stone!

❊ If you wear lilies of the valley on May 1 and make a wish, it's bound to come true. At least that's what many people in France believe.

✳ In Akita City, Japan, the Kanto Festival is held each year to invoke divine help for a good harvest. A *kanto* is a long bamboo pole with several horizontal ribs from which hang as many as 50 lanterns. The young men of the city try their skill at balancing kanto on their hands, foreheads, shoulders, and hips.

✳ In some areas of England, the people believe that the apple can help produce babies. So at certain times, young people join hands and dance around apple trees—hoping this will make them more prolific.

✳ Cornhuskings in rural parts of New Hampshire are still quite popular—especially among young people. Neighbors gather to help husk the corn. And the tradition is that if a girl finds a red ear—she can be kissed by the first man who can catch her**!**

✳ "Have a pretzel!" is not just a friendly expression in Luxembourg. They have a holiday called Pretzel Sunday. On this day, young men give young ladies cakes in pretzel form as a sign that they're interested in eventual marriage.

✳ The Aborigines of Australia had a unique method of getting fresh honey. They captured a bee, stuck a feather on it and then, using the marked bee as a guide, followed it to the hive.

✳ When you raise your glass at mealtime and drink to the health of your guest, you're following an ancient custom that really had to do with health!

Long ago, the host would raise his glass and drink first to show that the beverage was not harmful. This little ceremony would indicate to the guest that the host was friendly and wished him no harm. So when you toast your guest by raising a glass, you're observing the old custom of assuring him that it is all right for his health to drink what you served!

✳ Long hair on women is not just a matter of appearance in Sumatra. The women who sow the rice let their hair hang loose—to induce the rice to grow richly and have long stalks.

✳ Tattooing on the chin was a sign of high rank among the Maori of New Zealand. No longer practiced, it is nevertheless common among the elders.

✳ The Colorado Indians of Ecuador cover their bodies with an orange-red dye as a protection against evil spirits.

✳ That beauty is in the eye of the beholder is something everyone accepts by now. What people in another part of the world consider beautiful may be something we would consider quite ugly.

A rather extreme example of this is called cicatrization. It is a form of scar tattooing, and is still practiced by many tribal peoples. The skin is cut again and again in the same place so that when it finally heals, a raised scar remains. Tribesmen in Australia, for example, consider these scars very ornamental.

✳ People all over the world have different ways of identifying themselves. Members of the Luo tribe in Kenya take out six lower teeth at the front of the mouth.

✳ When the king or queen of England is to be present in the House of Lords, peers never show up with gloves on. This is a way of making certain that they will carry no hidden weapons. It's a precaution that goes back to the days when gloves were much larger—and plots against the monarch rather frequent.

✳ If you've ever been in a house where they pointed out "the drawing room"—you know it's not a room where drawing or painting is done.

It seems that during the sixteenth century in England, it became the custom for ladies and gentlemen to separate after dinner. The men remained in the dining room to drink and talk. The ladies went to a special room set aside for their gossip and talk.

What the ladies did was *withdraw*—and the room they went to came to be known as the withdrawing room. In time, this was shortened to the drawing room, which it is still called today.

❋ Don't step on a cat's tail—if you're an unmarried male. In certain parts of France people believe that a bachelor who does so won't find any woman willing to marry him for the next twelve months!

※ So many people in Wales have the same surnames, they have to find ways to set themselves apart. In one small Welsh village, there are so many Joneses that they refer to one another as Jones the Fish, Jones the Baker, Jones the Railway, etc. And the undertaker is Jones the Death.

❋ The "sun lunch" is part of the celebration in Greenland to greet the arrival of the sun. During the early part of winter there is no sun, only darkness. On the day the sun is due to appear again, the "sun lunch" is held—and the luncheon table is placed near a window so that the sunshine can come in as the honored guest!

❋ If you ever entertain British royalty, be sure there are no finger bowls on the dining table. It seems that back in the days when many people in England considered the exiled Catholic Stuarts the rightful claimants to the throne, they would drink the royal toast in a special way. They held their glasses over the finger bowls, symbolically drinking to "the king over the water," meaning "across the sea." It was considered an act of treason then, and it's still not proper to have finger bowls when the king or queen is present.

✻ Cutting the fingernails is part of appearing neat and proper. We may even do it before starting out on a trip. But not the Japanese. They believe the fingernails must never be cut before starting out on a journey—or it will bring disgrace to the person before he reaches his destination.

✻ Pin money is actually part of the history of women's lib. As far back as the fourteenth century, many people believed women shouldn't have money of their own to spend. In the fight against this, a husband would agree to give his bride a sum of money every year to spend on anything she wished. Since it would usually be spent on clothing and ornaments to go on clothing—and since pins were just being introduced—it came to be known as pin money.

✳ In hot climates, perspiration is good for the body, and a dry skin is an indication of fever. So in Cairo, many people greet each other with the salutation "How do you sweat?"

✳ Everybody knows about Big Ben, the bell in the clock tower of the Houses of Parliament in London. But why is it called Big Ben? It was originally called St. Stephen's Bell. The commissioner of works, Sir Benjamin Hall, had much to do with putting up the new Houses of Parliament in 1851. He was an enormous man, and folks called him Big Ben. When the question came up in Parliament what to name the great bell that was to be hung in the tower, a member yelled out, "Why not call it Big Ben?"—and the name stuck.

❊ The most unusual commuters in the world are Turks who make a ten-minute ferry trip every day. They go across the Bosporus from Üsküdar to Istanbul. In those ten minutes, they actually commute from one continent, Asia, to another, Europe!

❊ With the globalization of film, television, and all kinds of communication, customs, clothing styles, and even food are becoming more and more alike all over the world.

One of the things that people in Europe and America have taught the rest of the world is to kiss! The Chinese didn't have the custom of kissing. Neither did the Japanese. In Samoa, the kiss is really a sniff. The Polynesians—and the Eskimo—rub noses together.

So the kiss, as a form of affection, actually developed rather late in human history. But it seems to be here to stay.

✻ In certain countries, different dialects are spoken in different sections. But in India, while Hindi and English are the chief official languages, *hundreds* of other languages are spoken. In fact, a great many Indians cannot understand Indians from another part of their country at all!

✻ The natives of southeast Alaska long ago discovered that the eulachon, a smeltlike, fatty fish, makes a perfect candle after it has been dried and threaded with a wick. The smell is evil but the light is fine.

Entertainment

One of Austria's greatest collectors of art was Emperor Rudolf II, a seventeenth-century ruler who spent so much money on art that his court was frequently put on short rations.

Emperor Rudolf's favorite artist was a man named Savery, who painted a famous picture called *Landscape with Birds*.

This canvas was done in 1628 and shows a dodo bird, a big, awkward creature, unable to fly, who then lived on the island of Mauritius in the Indian Ocean.

Savery's painting of the dodo was the only one ever done from a living dodo, so some years later when the dodo became extinct, Savery's painting of the bird was widely copied.

But Savery had made one mistake. For some reason, he painted the dodo with two right feet. And ever since then all the artists who have copied Savery's dodo have continued to make the same structural error.

So the poor, clumsy dodo bird, gone from this earth for centuries, must go down through posterity with two right feet!

✳ Every year, the Academy of Motion Picture Arts and Sciences awards a trophy to people who have made an outstanding contribution to cinema. The trophy—a golden statuette—is officially called the Academy Award of Merit. According to legend, an employee named Margaret Herrick spotted the award and said, "Why, he looks just like my uncle Oscar." Since then, the awards ceremony and the statuettes have been called the Oscars.

✳ It's a complete Dutch city, and it has everything: canals, railroads, ships that move, stores, and factories. But it's actually a miniature, scaled to ⅟₂₅ of actual size. And it can be seen in the park at Madurodam, just outside The Hague, in Holland.

❋ In 1609, an English ship, the *Sea Venture*, under the command of Sir George Somers, set out on a voyage to the New World.

Caught in a violent storm, the little vessel was wrecked on the coast of Bermuda. The crew managed to make shore safely. Then, from the wrecked timbers of their ship, they made two small boats and sailed across the water to Virginia, where they decided to settle.

But the hard, primitive life on the Virginia coast disappointed these early settlers, and they decided to return to Bermuda.

Shortly after their return, Sir George Somers died. His son buried his father's heart in Bermuda and then sailed back to England with the body.

This very romantic story of the storm, the

shipwreck, and the death of Somers proved a sensation in London, and a popular playwright decided to write about the adventure.

The play became one of the most famous and enduring of all time, for the writer was William Shakespeare and the play was *The Tempest.*

❋ Flower arranging is considered a great art by the Japanese. And flowers play an important role in Japanese social occasions. But you will never see orchids, gentians, daphnes, or azaleas at a happy event. These flowers are prohibited by custom from use at happy occasions!

❋ Back in the 1700s a new dance hit Vienna. It paired off dancers in wildly revolving couples and was the opposite of the slow minuet.

Overnight, the lively dance became a city-wide craze. Huge ballrooms sprang up by the dozens; their doors were never closed and mobs of eager dancers surged in at all hours. Rotating orchestras played around the clock. Intoxicated by the dance, people neglected their work, abandoned their children, left their sick untended.

And what was the dance that had turned the Austrian capital into a city of madness? It wasn't a Disco-style dance. It wasn't St. Vitus's dance. Would you believe it was the waltz?

✲ There is nothing "special" about a small atoll called Tetiaroa, which is just north of Tahiti. Except perhaps, that it was owned by movie star Marlon Brando, who wanted to use it for sportfishing. And that's a long way to go for the sport, considering that Tetiaroa is roughly 3,720 miles from Los Angeles, 2,416 miles from Honolulu, and 3,500 miles from Sydney—the only cities from which you can fly there!

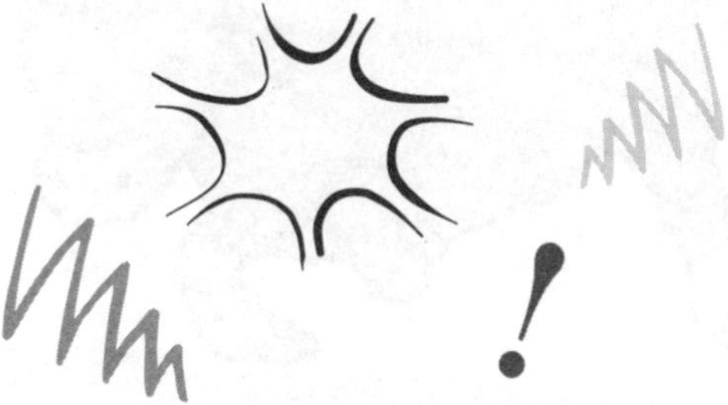

✳ The color red is said to be irritating to a bull. The animal is thought to become especially enraged when a red object—a piece of cloth, for example—is moved about.

Actually, bulls cannot see colors. While not all animals have as yet been tested for color blindness, it is believed that humans, apes, and monkeys are the only mammals able to see color.

If the bull does not become enraged at the sight of red cloth, why is it used in bull-fighting? The bullfighter, whether he is aware of it or not, is waving around the red cape more to excite the audience than to excite the bull. Human beings are very responsive to the color red. It is a bright color; it is the color of blood; it is a color associated with danger.

As for the bull, what excites him is not the color of the cloth, but its motion. Waving a green towel or a pair of yellow pajamas would excite him just about as much.

✳ The Colosseum in Rome was used for gladiatorial combats and public spectacles, as everybody knows. But how long was it the scene for such performances? It was opened in 80 CE—and the shows went on for 400 years!

✳ "The Star-Spangled Banner" was written by Francis Scott Key (1779–1843) during the War of 1812 and thereafter was often played on patriotic occasions. But it did not become the official national anthem of the United States until almost 120 years later, on March 3, 1931, when Congress proclaimed it as such.

Furthermore, it is not widely known that Francis Scott Key wrote only the words of the song. Ironically, the tune of "The Star-Spangled Banner " was taken from "To Anacreon in Heaven," an English drinking song!

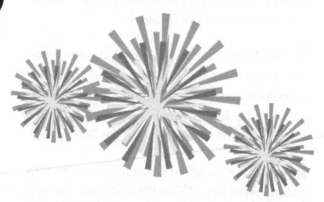

❋ Everything about *Noh* drama, a form of theater in Japan, is traditional: the music, the costumes and masks the actors wear—even the gestures they make. When an actor wants to indicate he is crying, he just raises his hand toward his face—and everyone in the audience understands that he's crying!

❋ Mountaineers in southern Poland have a dangerous dance called the *Zbojnicki*. During the dance, a young man swings an ax in a circular motion a few inches from the floor—and a young lady has to jump over it as it goes around. If she misses a step . . . **!**

❋ If you are sometimes tempted to complain about the service in a hotel, consider this: In 1836, the Astor House opened in New York and offered a sensational service available for the first time—hot running water on the first floor**!**

❋ The numerals we use are called Arabic numerals. But they weren't invented by the Arabs at all! The Hindu scholars in ancient India invented the numerals. It was because the Arabs introduced them to the Western world that they got their name.

Sports

If you like to play chess, you should see the way they play in Marostica, Italy. There is an immense chessboard built into the public square. The pawns and all the pieces are human beings. And the knights sit on real horses!

✳ Mickey Mantle, one of the greatest baseball players ever, was "discovered" by a fireman. This fireman, who lived in Commerce,

Oklahoma, tipped off a Yankee scout about Mantle, then a kid playing in the Ban Johnson League. Mickey was signed up by Yankee scout Tony Greenwade, while they sat in the backseat of a car on a rainy Sunday afternoon. The rest is baseball history**!**

✳ Although the football is sometimes referred to as a pigskin, it is not made of pigskin. It is made of cowhide.

✳ Kite flying is a popular sport in Malaysia. The kites are designed to resemble birds, fish, cats, and human beings. Bright colors add beauty to the designs. The kites are also used in competition, and the kite attaining the greatest height above the ground is declared the winner.

✳ Hockey is generally a low-scoring game. As a matter of fact, the feat of one player scoring three or more goals in a single game is rare enough to have a designation all its own—the hat trick, a name reputedly derived from the offer of a felt hat by a Canadian hat manufacturer to any player who managed the achievement.

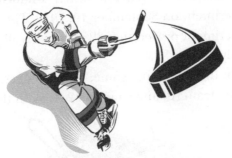

✳ In 1980, a quarter-mile race called the Elephantonian was held at New York's Monticello Raceway. The race matched a six-year-old, 3,000-pound elephant against an eight-year-old, 3,500-pound elephant named Nellie. Who won? Tusk, Tusk! The results were never reported.

✻ The average nine-inning major league baseball game today requires about 2 hours and 45 minutes to complete. However, a game can be played much faster, as was proved by the Southern Association, which conducted an experiment on September 19, 1910. The experiment proved that 32 minutes is all you really need.

In this 32-minute game, Mobile edged the home team Atlanta Crackers 2–1. With the

score tied 1–1 in the first half of the ninth, Mobile pushed across the decisive run. Both teams hustled every minute of the way. Batters did not wait out the pitchers but swung at every good pitch. There was only one walk; not a single player struck out; and Mobile even reeled off a triple play. Mobile made 6 hits against 4 for Atlanta. On the same afternoon, Chattanooga at Nashville needed only 42 minutes to complete all nine innings.

✳ Soccer, polo, cricket, field hockey, tennis: The favorite sports of what country? India! The reason, of course, is that the British rule over India left love of these sports as one of its legacies.

✳ When football was first being played in American colleges, there were so many injuries and accidents that Harvard University decided to forbid it. So on July 2, 1860, a football funeral was held. "Football Fightum," an effigy, was put into a coffin and buried in a grave by the sophomore class. But on the tombstone was written: "It will rise again"—and it certainly did!

❋ The ball game that came before other ball games (such as tennis, baseball, and football) was handball. In Italy it was called *pallone*, in France *jeu de paume*, and in England *fives*. Why fives? Because the ball was struck by the hand—a "bunch of fives."

❋ Married men wrestle against bachelors in Brazil, as part of a ceremonial dance. The unmarried men, dressed in feathery leggings and sleeves, line up to challenge their married brothers to wrestle.

❋ Bowling is a popular sport in America, but don't bet on it. Betting on the game of bowling almost finished it as a sport. In the 1840s, Connecticut lawmakers banned it because too much gambling went on when people bowled. To stop the gambling, nine-pin bowling was made illegal. To get around the law, bowlers added a tenth pin so they could bowl without breaking the law. Bowling has been using ten pins ever since.

✳ One of the contests in the herdsmen's festival in Switzerland is the throwing of a 185-pound, egg-shaped granite boulder. The dates on the rock commemorate the first *Unspunnen* Festival and its 100th anniversary.

✳ In Turkey, camel wrestling is a major sporting event, especially in the area around the Aegean Sea. The big humpback animals actually engage in a long shoving match, with an occasional bite thrown in to get the opponent to move off. The camels are never badly hurt, and the winner is the camel who simply doesn't give up.

✳ In the early days of football, the game did not have a lot of standard rules. Originally, there was no rule governing how many players could actively participate on each side. Before a game, the two teams involved decided how many players would be on the field at one time; as many as 25 players on each side played in early football contests. It wasn't until 1876 that a rule was established limiting each team to just 15 players on the field. Finally, in 1880 the rule was changed to allow teams the use of only 11 players at a time.

※ The pre-Columbian Aztecs in Mexico played a game similar to basketball that they called *ollamalitzil*. Players tried to put a solid rubber ball through a hole in a fixed stone placed high on the side of a stadium wall. Losing a game of *ollamalitzil* was costly:

> The captain of the losing squad was often beheaded and the winning team was entitled to the clothing of all of the spectators as a prize for being victorious.

※ Pro boxers Willie Pep and Willie Pastrano shared a superstition:—They both believed it was good luck to tie their wedding rings to their shoelaces for a prizefight.

✻ A big thrill for visitors to Greenland is a ride on a dogsled. How fast can they go? On good firm ground, with a team of 10 dogs— only about 12 miles an hour.

✻ A crazy old baseball superstition concerned empty beer barrels. Baseball players of the past believed that seeing a truckload of empty beer barrels going by before a game was good luck and guaranteed a team would get a lot of hits. To take advantage of that silly superstition, manager John McGraw of the New York Giants once secretly hired a man to drive a truck filled with empty beer barrels past his team as the players entered the stadium for a crucial series against the Chicago Cubs. McGraw's trick worked, as the truck rolled past the Giant players before each contest of the four-game series. However, the secret was uncovered after the series' end, when the truck driver showed up at the stadium looking to be paid for services rendered.

✳ Who invented cheerleaders? Many sports historians believe the first cheerleaders were used by Princeton University in 1869 and 1870. In 1869, Princeton and Rutgers Universities met in New Jersey to play the first college football game in history. Part of Princeton's team strategy was to have its players yell loudly during the game to distract and frighten the opposition. The strategy didn't quite work, as Princeton lost that first game in 1869. All that yelling also wore out the Princeton players. However, the next year, the team brought a special group of spectators to the contest to do the yelling and cheering for them. In 1870, with the help of its special "cheerleaders," Princeton defeated Rutgers on the gridiron.

❋ A real contest of strength is one of the events at the Braemar Games held in Scotland. It is called "tossing the caber." It consists of throwing the roughly trimmed trunk of a young tree as far as possible!

✳ A college professor can be excused for being absentminded, but not a big league umpire during the course of a ball game. Because Vic Delmore became absentminded at a St. Louis Cardinals–Chicago Cubs game played at Wrigley Field on June 30, 1959, he caused one of the strangest and most bizarre plays in baseball history.

The Cards' top hitter, Stan Musial, was at bat with a 3–1 count when the next pitch got away from Cub catcher Sammy Taylor and skidded toward the backstop.

Umpire Delmore called ball four and Musial trotted toward first. But Taylor and pitcher Bob Anderson argued vehemently with the ump that it was a foul tip.

Since the ball was still in play and Taylor had not chased it, Musial ran toward second. Fast-thinking third baseman Alvin Dark then raced to the backstop and retrieved the ball. Meanwhile, Delmore was still involved in the argument with the Cub battery mates when he unthinkingly pulled a second ball out of his pocket and handed it to catcher Taylor. Suddenly noticing Musial dashing for second, pitcher Anderson grabbed the new ball and threw to second—at the same time that Dark threw to shortstop Ernie Banks with the original ball!

Anderson's throw sailed over second base into center field. Musial saw the ball fly past his head, so—not realizing there were two balls in play—he took off for third only to run smack into Banks, who tagged him out with the original ball.

After a lengthy conference, the umpires ruled that Musial was out since he was tagged with the original ball.

Also ruled out was Vic Delmore himself. Citing a lack of confidence in Vic, National League President Warren Giles fired him at season's end.

❊ The Chicago White Sox really stuck together in 1940. Everyone on the team had exactly the same batting average before and after opening day in 1940. That was because Bob Feller of the Cleveland Indians pitched a no-hitter and every Chicago player ended up with a .000 average until the next game.

❋ Pro baseball player Minnie Minoso, of the Chicago White Sox, blamed his batting slump during a doubleheader on "evil spirits" in his uniform. To get rid of the bad spirits, Minoso took a shower while wearing his uniform and washed away the evil. In the next game, Minoso got three hits—two of them home runs!

❋ The final resting place of William Ambrose Hulbert, who helped found baseball's National League, is in Chicago near Wrigley Field. The tombstone is in the shape of a large baseball.

❋ One of the world's most popular sports, so the story goes, was started by a British schoolboy. At Rugby School in 1823, William Webb Ellis was playing in a soccer game when he picked up the ball and ran with it. This was illegal, but it led to the start of a new ball game—rugby.

✳ When you want to move the ball down the court in basketball, you can either dribble or pass. Many years ago, basketball players did not have that choice. Why not? Dribbling in basketball was once an illegal maneuver. When the game was invented in 1891, only passing was allowed. It wasn't until around 1900 that a rule change made dribbling legal.

✳ Twice a year, the natives of the Fijis stage what they call a *vara wai*, an unusual fishing expedition into the inlets of the area. It is designed to gather ordinary fish and also to rid the waters of the vicious sharks that lurk there.

Using bamboo, the natives weave a long fencelike net to be used as a trap. They anchor one end of this on the near shore and then move the other end out across the water.

Once they have reached the opposite shore, they work the free end back toward the anchored end in a large arc, thus trapping thousands of fish in the shallow water within the corral that is formed by the net.

Dinner is now just a step away, but there remain the sharks to be gotten rid of. For included in those teeming thousands of fish within the net are sometimes dozens of sharks.

Moreover, there's only one way to get them out of that corral, and that's to get in there with them.

Certain islanders—specially trained just for that purpose—wade into the mass of trapped fish, searching for the sharks. When they find one, they lean over and catch him with their bare hands. Then, turning the shark on his back, they plant a solid kiss on his belly. This quiets him immediately.

Why sharks react as they do this strange treatment is a mystery. Whether the kiss conveys some kind of special power, or whether the place where the kiss is planted immobilizes the sharks, no one seems to know. But from the time they are kissed, the sharks show no further signs of life and they are then disposed of easily.

❊ At the racetrack at Marka, which is just outside Amman, the capital of Jordan, they not only have horse races—they also have camel races! The racing camels are a very special breed, light and slender, and they can go very fast.

❊ How popular a sport is soccer in some countries? Consider the case of Denmark. It has a population of about 5 million people. And there are 12,000 soccer clubs in the country— with about 457,000 Danes as members!

Whenever Sweden— Denmark's greatest

rival—manages to defeat the Danish soccer team, the whole country is plunged into gloom!

❉ Waterskiing is a popular sport in many tropical countries. In Austria they have a sport called *skijoring* that is a land version of that. The skiers are pulled across snow-covered roads by riders on horseback!

❉ Every sport has strange twists in its records books, but one of the strangest of all belongs to baseball.

In Allentown, Pennsylvania, in 1893, a 2–2 game was in the last of the 11th inning. Nail-biting suspense gripped the crowd as Cincinnati came to bat, determined to break the deadlock and post a hard-earned victory.

Cincinnati's leadoff batter was retired, and the next batter, "Matches" Kilroy, took a couple of pitches, then swung mightily and grounded out to the infield.

There still was that all-important third out remaining, and manager "King" Kelly, one of Cincinnati's best hitters, was due to bat next.

But Kilroy's futile effort apparently had created an insurmountable problem, for, in grounding out, he had split the last available bat.

Umpire Tim Durst, one of the most famous and respected of the period, pondered the situation for a few moments and then decided the game would have to be called because, without a bat, there seemed to be no possible way to continue.

He beckoned the two managers to his side and began his explanation. Kelly shook his head and asked Durst to postpone his ruling, arguing he would find a bat somehow.

Noticing a woodpile nearby. Kelly raced over to it, searching for something he could use to swing at the ball. He found an ax and hurried back to the diamond.

"I'll use this to bat," he proclaimed.

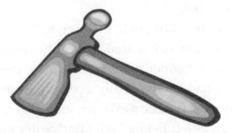

Durst shook his head in disbelief.

"Show me in the rule book where it's illegal," Kelly insisted.

Durst began searching through the book. He turned page after page of the small volume, shaking his head as he continued. Finally Durst straightened up, stuffed the book into his back pocket, and shouted, "Play ball." There was nothing in the rules to prohibit the use of an ax as a bat.

The triumphant manager swaggered into the batter's box, hefted his ax, and waited. Twice the pitcher threw, and twice Kelly swung, meeting only air as he struggled with his strange bat.

On the third pitch, however, Kelly connected. The ball soared toward the fence in left field. Suddenly, without warning, the ball, which had been partially separated by the ax blade and further weakened in its flight, split in half as left fielder "Wild Bill" Setley followed its course.

Stunned, Setley watched as half of the ball flew over the fence behind and half dropped at his feet.

Uncertain of what to do, he looked toward the infield and saw Kelly racing around the

bases. Quickly Setley recovered, snatched up the half of the ball lying in front of him, and threw it toward the plate. The runner and the ball converged.

From the stands thundered the excited cry of the fans, "Slide, Kelly! Slide!" a phrase that has survived through the succeeding years.

Responding to his encouragement, Kelly slid but the catcher grabbed the ball, whirled, and tagged the Cincinnati captain an instant before he reached home.

Leaping to his feet, Kelly charged the confused umpire, who was about to signal him out.

Durst recognized he was going to get an argument and calmly pointed out that Kelly's slide had not beaten the throw.

"Okay, I agree," Kelly said, "but how about the half of the ball that went over the fence? I wasn't tagged with the whole ball."

This was a line of reasoning that Durst was not prepared for and, as he hesitated, a long and heated debate began. No matter how he ruled, Durst realized he stood to lose.

Finally, with the wisdom of Solomon, the umpire stepped back, quieted the adversaries, and announced that he was awarding a half run to Cincinnati. At the same time, he was charging them with a half out.

Thus the strangest score of all time ended a baseball game. Cincinnati was declared the winner—2½ to 2.

✳ When the game of basketball was invented in 1891, there were no "basketballs," so soccer balls were used to play the game. It wasn't until

1894 that a special basketball was introduced. A "laceless" basketball came into use in 1937, and the modern basketball appeared in 1950.

✳ Historian believe the ancient Egyptians enjoyed the sport of bowling. Pieces of stone used as pins and a stone ball used to knock them down were found in the tomb of an Egyptian child.

✳ The Olympic Games have produced more than their share of unusual sports stories and political beefs, but maybe none so strange as the saga of Wyndham Halswelle.

Halswelle, one of England's premier quarter-milers, won the 400-meter race in 1908 when the Games were staged in his native country. But he had to run the distance twice, and the second time he ran it alone.

Unlike today, when literally dozens of runners enter this popular event, there were only four men entered in the 400-meter race in 1908.

Three were Americans. The fourth was Halswelle, and he was far and away the favorite of the crowd. The members of the American trio were considered intruders, hardly fit to set foot upon the same track as the popular Englishman.

But when the starting gun barked, the four men sprinted away almost as one. In the first and second turns and down the back stretch they battled it out head-to-head.

Finally, the flying quartet rounded the final turn and headed toward the tape, almost shoulder to shoulder.

Suddenly, one of the American runners, a Cornell University sprinter named Carpenter, burst from the pack and charged into the lead.

Almost at the same instant, one of the officials gathered near the finish line leaped out onto the track, threw both hands above his head, and shouted, "Foul!"

Seconds later Carpenter breasted the tape, closely followed by a second American sprinter and then by Halswelle, a disappointing third.

But as the participants returned to the finish line, the officials gathered in a tight little knot, discussing the actions of the judge. Before the group could disperse, Halswelle shouldered his way close and lodged the complaint that he had been jostled coming out of the last turn.

While the spectators and runners waited for the officials' decision, a tense silence settled over the stadium. The discussion went on for several minutes, and then the four runners were called to the group of officials to hear the decision.

"We have decided to allow Mr. Halswelle's protest," a spokesman said. "However, we have been unable to decide which runner was responsible for the foul. Therefore, we order the race rerun."

The three Americans shook their heads. Carpenter spoke up on their behalf.

"We cannot agree with your decision. We feel that if a foul was committed, the guilty runner alone should be punished, and the rest of the results should stand. If you insist upon running the race over, we will not participate."

But the judges' minds were not to be changed. They ordered the runners to return to the starting line, and set a time limit for their appearance.

When that time limit had expired, only Halswelle stood at the starting line. Then, with the stunned spectators looking on, the formality of an official start was carried out and Halswelle sped around the track, rerunning the 400-meter race all by himself.

He was declared the official winner of the event for the 1908 Olympic Games, the only time in history a one-man race determined a gold medal.

Ironically, Halswelle posted a time of 50 seconds flat. Never since and only once before in the history of that event has any man ever won the 400-meter race in slower time than that. His achievement still ranks as one of the strangest in the long history of the modern Olympic Games.

❋ Just for luck, pro tennis player Art Larsen used to talk to an imaginary eagle that he said was

perched on his right shoulder during matches. The bird supposedly brought him good luck.

✳ In 1945, William Sianis put a hex on the Chicago Cubs baseball team because the club wouldn't let Sianis bring his pet goat into Wrigley Field for a World Series game. The hex was supposed to keep the Cubs from ever winning a pennant. In 1981, William Sianis's son Sam finally lifted the hex. Why? The Cubs invited Sam to attend a game at Wrigley Field along with a goat named Billy, who was the mascot of the popular Chicago tavern owned by the Sianis family. It was all part of a clever publicity stunt.

✳ Would you believe that Olympic track immortal Jessie Owens once raced a horse? It's true. When Owens decided to become a professional runner, he raced a horse named Julio McCaw at a racetrack in Havana, Cuba, as a publicity stunt. The race turned out to be funny to everyone but the horse. Owens was awarded a 40-yard handicap in the 100-yard race—and won! The last laugh was on Julio McCaw.

✳ The game of golf was so popular in Scotland during the fifteenth century that King James II was afraid it would replace archery in popularity among his people. Since archery was necessary for national defense, the king outlawed the sport, and it wasn't until 1502 that it was legal to play golf in Scotland once again.

✳ Donnybrook is a suburb of Dublin where an annual fair was held for more than 600 years. The fair was discontinued in 1855 due to the violet brawls that always broke out while it was going on. The word *Donnybrook* is now a synonym for *brawl.*

✳ Ouch! Prior to 1914, hockey officials were required to *place* the puck down on the ice between players' sticks for face-offs. More often than not, officials ended up with bruised hands, cut fingers, and broken bones. To spare them some pain, a rule was finally passed in 1914 that allowed them to simply drop the puck between the sticks of players for face-offs.

History

It's often said that history repeats itself. But this saying has never been more dramatically borne out than in the striking similarities found in the assassinations of Abraham Lincoln and John F. Kennedy:

Abraham Lincoln was elected President in 1860; John Kennedy was elected exactly a century later, in 1960.

Lincoln was warned not to attend Ford's Theater on the night he was shot; Kennedy was warned not to visit Dallas.

Both men where shot on a Friday, in public view, while sitting happily and at ease beside their wives. Both were shot from behind, the fatal bullet in each case entering the back of the head.

The men who succeeded Lincoln and Kennedy to the presidency were both named Johnson. Andrew Johnson was born in 1808; Lyndon Baines Johnson was born in 1908.

Both Johnsons were Democrats, Southerners, and former Senators.

John Wilkes Booth shot Lincoln in a theater and was later found in a tobacco storage barn, or warehouse; Lee Harvey Oswald shot Kennedy from a book storage warehouse and was found in a movie theater.

Both assassins were shot down before they could be brought to trial.

※ In Alaska, when it was still a Russian possession, there was a tribe of Indians called the Tlingit. They carved totem poles. When Abraham Lincoln was president of the United States, they carved a huge wooden likeness of him. It can be seen now in a museum in Juneau.

※ A collection that begins as a hobby can become quite important. Thomas Jefferson was a great collector of books. His collection was so fine that it eventually became the nucleus of the Library of Congress, after the original holdings of the library were destroyed by fire in 1814. Incidentally, there are now more than 29 million books in the Library of Congress.

✳ A Washington museum in England? Yes! It's Sulgrave Manor in Northamptonshire. It was George Washington's family's home, and it has been restored and refurnished and made into a museum.

✳ Because all modern presidents were born citizens of the United States, it is widely assumed that all presidents were natural-born citizens. Actually, the first seven presidents were not born U.S. citizens, but British subjects. When these presidents were born, to put it simply, there was no such thing as the United States. Martin Van Buren (1837–41), the eighth president, was the first U.S.–born president.

The U.S. Constitution requires that "No Person except a natural born Citizen, or a

Citizen of the United States, at the time of the Adoption of this Constitution, shall be eligible to the Office of President." Once the Constitution was ratified, unless they declined citizenship (which many Loyalists did), all former British subjects automatically became citizens of the United States. The first seven presidents were thus granted citizenship and became eligible for the office.

✻ Alexander the Great, who lived about 2,300 years ago, ordered all his soldiers to shave their heads and faces. This prevented an enemy from grabbing a soldier by the hair to cut his head off.

✳ During World War II, a young man entered an enlistment center and eagerly asked to join the service. He said his name was Kincaid, he was 21 years old, and he wanted to become a flyer.

He was accepted into the Air Force and after training in the United States he was assigned to a bomber squadron at the Benghazi air base in North Africa.

As a gunner on a B-24 bomber, Kincaid soon ran up a terrific record, was decorated, and was made a sergeant.

Then one day his buddy was killed, and so deeply did his friend's death affect the young airman that he asked for a transfer.

The transfer was granted. The flyer returned to the United States and immediately went to see his commanding officer. His name, he told the astonished officer, was not Kincaid, it was Fletcher, and he was not 21 years old, as his military record stated, but only 16. He had been only 15 when he had enlisted the year before, and he had lied then about both his name and age.

Tom Fletcher was the youngest combat flyer in World War II. At the age of 16 he was already a veteran. He had completed 35 combat missions, had flown 300 combat flying hours, had won the Distinguished Flying Cross, and had been given the Air Medal with one silver cluster and 5 bronze clusters.

✳ The Pennsylvania Dutch—a community of religious people who live in a simple way in eastern Pennsylvania—are not Dutch but German. The sect has been misnamed, perhaps because the German word *Deutsch*, meaning "German," was confused with "Dutch" by people unfamiliar with the German language.

✳ Did you know that the Nobel Peace Prize was named after Alfred B. Nobel? They irony of that is Mr. Nobel was the inventor of dynamite, which caused the death of millions of soldiers in wars all over the world.

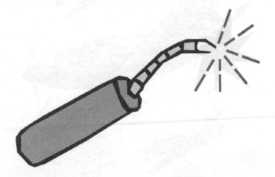

✳ Wine tasters had a dangerous job in the fifteenth century—they tested for the presence of poison, not the quality of the beverage.

✳ One of the names that leaps from the pages of Egyptian history is that of Hatshepsut, who ruled from 1501 to 1479 BCE.

There's a difference between Hatshepsut and her predecessors, however: Hatshepsut was a woman.

Sacred tradition in ancient Egypt required that every ruler must be a son of the great god Amon. Thus, at least in theory, Hatshepsut could not rule Egypt. And, even for someone as capable and strong-willed as this daughter of Thutmose I, first king of the Eighteenth Dynasty, this was a tradition that could not be ignored.

Hatshepsut was raised to partnership on the throne of Egypt by her father, Thutmose I, as he neared the end of his 30-year reign. But because tradition decreed she could not succeed him, when he died, Hatshepsut's half brother, who was also her husband, became King Thutmose II.

In turn, before Thutmose II died, he named Thutmose III an obscure son of Thutmose I whose mother had been a concubine, to succeed him. That move was too much for Hatshepsut to swallow, and she promptly seized the throne for herself.

To justify her move, she invented a biography that, to her satisfaction at least, solved the problem of her sex.

In the biography, Hatshepsut wrote that Amon had descended from his heaven and impregnated her mother, Ahmasi. As he departed, he announced that the fruit of the union would be female but that all of his strength and valor would flow through her to the Egyptian people.

Then, as if in further justification, when she appeared in public, Hatshepsut dressed in male clothing and sported a false beard. In later years, she had herself represented on the many monuments she raised as a bearded, breastless warrior.

Pointless as the masquerade may have been, it satisfied both Hatshepsut and her subjects and kept Thutmose III from the throne for almost 22 years.

Hatshepsut left her mark on Egypt. Before her death, she built for herself a secret and ornate tomb on the western side of the Nile, across from the then-capital of Thebes. In succeeding generations, more than 60 of the rulers who followed her would build royal sepulchers in Hatshepsut's city of the dead. Eventually, the collection became known as the Valley of the Kings' Tombs.

※ Primitive man knew of poisons from his own daily experience. He thought that demons lived in the roots of plants and, when displeased, these demons would take revenge by inflicting madness, delirium or death on the offender. As far as he could tell the demons were easily aroused, because everywhere he looked, his comrades were dying of mysterious causes. What is understandable to the modern mind, which is familiar with the variety of poisonous nuts, berries, mushrooms and plants and the necessity for proper food preparation, was terrifying to our ignorant forefathers.

So primitive man felt a deep need for something he could invest with spiritual powers to protect him from the beasts and the demons. Amulets and talismans were such divinely endowed objects. The first amulets and talismans had three main missions: to get the "demon" out of the afflicted person, to ward off evil, and to sway other spirits to do favors. These first primeval amulets were simple things: necklaces or pendants of bears' claws or oddly shaped rocks, perhaps blood red or purple. Then, as time went on, the complexity of the amulets increased. They became more like ornate jewelry and, at the same time, each became associated with a ritual. Each disease required not only the right amulet but the right ritual—the words and actions to go with that amulet. At first ordinary men could manage, but soon these

rituals required the services of a specialist. This was the origin of the witch doctor, medicine man, shaman, and other spiritual practitioner.

✳ The last prisoner to be kept in the Tower of London—where Sir Walter Raleigh, Mary Queen of Scots, and Lady Jane Grey were once prisoners—was Rudolf Hess, the Nazi leader. He parachuted into England and was jailed in the Tower of London during World War II.

✻ Did St. Patrick really rid Ireland of snakes? To this day, there are no snakes in Ireland. And, by the way, there are only two kinds of mice to be found in this country, which is also unusual. The natives don't mind the lack of these creatures at all.

✻ The 16-year-old girl was named Sybil Ludington. She lived on a farm near New York with her father, who was a captain in the militia.

On the night of April 27, 1777, a messenger arrived with urgent news for Sybil's father. The British, in a surprise attack from Long Island Sound, had burned the city of Danbury, Connecticut, and were advancing on the countryside. Every farmer needed to be called out immediately.

Because her father was captain of the militia, Sybil volunteered for the job of calling the farmers to fight.

Grabbing a big stick, the girl leaped on her horse and galloped off in the darkness. All night long she rode, pausing at each farmhouse only to crash her stick against the door and shout a warning: "The British are coming, fall out and fight."

Sybil Ludington far outdid Paul Revere's famous ride. Revere had traveled only about ten miles when he was captured by the British at Lexington. Sybil covered a staggering 40 miles of hard riding. What's more, she mustered out enough men to send the British back to their boats in defeat.

✻ The first time Christopher Columbus ever set foot on continental America (not on one of the islands) was on his third voyage, in 1498. Where did that happen? In Venezuela, at a point now called Cristobal Colón.

✻ Americans cherish their Liberty Bell as a symbol of their battle for freedom. So they gave the people of West Berlin a replica of the Liberty Bell to symbolize *their* struggle for freedom. It hangs in Schönberg Town Hall and is called the Freedom Bell.

❄ The huge Christ of the Andes that stands on the mountain frontier between Chile and Argentina is a symbol of peace between the two countries. And to dramatize that point, it was cast in bronze that was obtained from a cannon that had been used by the soldiers of Chile and Argentina.

❄ The old Greek word for copper was *kypros*—and that's how Cyprus got its name. They were mining copper in Cyprus thousands of years ago, and there seems to be no end to it. There are still rich deposits of it on the island today.

❄ The Forest of Martyrs near Jerusalem has 6 million trees. Each tree is a memorial to a Jewish life lost during the Holocaust.

❄ Did beer play an important part in deciding American history? Well, it has something to do with the decision of the Pilgrim

Fathers on the *Mayflower* to land at Plymouth Rock rather than continue to Virginia, where they had intended to make their home. In their journal is the following: "We could not now take time for further search or considerations, our victuals being very spent, especially our beer." By the way, they called it beer, but it was really ale that they drank.

✳ In 1882, the French secured the right to build a canal across Panama. When the project failed, a young French engineer named Bunau-Varilla tried to interest the United States.

The Americans were interested in a canal, but not across Panama. They wanted it to go across Nicaragua. Rejecting Bunau-Varilla's plea, Congress decided to vote funds for the Nicaraguan Canal.

But they did not take into account the resourceful Frenchman. Racing against time, Varilla wrote a letter to every congressman. And in each letter he enclosed a very interesting stamp. The stamp was from Nicaragua, and it showed one of that country's small volcanoes in full eruption.

As Varilla had suspected, the message came through loud and clear. The Congressmen read the letters, took a long look at the stamp—and then promptly reversed themselves. It was obvious that the United States could not build a canal through a country of active volcanoes.

In 1904, the United States bought the canal rights from the French. After years of incredible hardships the great engineering project was finally completed. On August 15, 1914, the first ship made its historic passage through the Panama Canal.

And the reason it crossed the isthmus at Panama instead of at Nicaragua was due to the picture of a volcano on an obscure stamp.

❋ The Battle of Bunker Hill was fought not on Bunker Hill but on nearby Breed's Hill, on June 17, 1775. This is why the monument commemorating the Battle of Bunker Hill is located on Breed's Hill.

Moreover, the Battle of Bennington, an important early victory of the American forces during the Revolution, was not fought in Bennington, Vermont; it took place near Walloomsac, New York, four miles northwest of

Bennington, on August 16, 1777. The battle was so named because it happened after British troops were sent by General John Burgoyne to Bennington to seize desperately needed supplies stored there. Before they could reach Bennington, however, the 1,400 British and Hessian troops were met near Walloomsac and defeated by 2,600 untrained American militia under General John Stark.

✳ Today, the whole world regards the Parthenon in Athens as probably the master-piece of Greek architecture. It was built about 447 BCE in honor of Athena. But this building wasn't always so honored. In the sixth century, the Christians used it as a church. Later, it was used as a mosque, and a minaret was actually added. And in the seventeenth century, the Turks used it to store their gunpowder!

❋ The marathon is named after a flat area in Greece where the ancient Persians and Greeks fought. A messenger bearing the news of the Greek victory ran from the battlefield at Marathon to Athens, a distance of 26 miles and 385 yards—the exact length of the modern race.

❋ Jerusalem is an ancient city, and the oldest map we have of it is on a wall in Madaba, Jordan. It is a mosaic picture map of the Holy City, with inscriptions in Greek characters, and it dates from the sixth century CE.

❋ A magnificently carved pillar stands in Rosslyn Chapel, Midlothian, in Scotland. It is called Prentice Pillar, and has a sad tale behind it. An apprentice is said to have carved it when his master was away. When the master returned and saw how beautiful it was, he killed the apprentice out of jealousy. But the pillar is named after the "prentice."

✳ Key West is a lovely island, and everybody assumes that the name has to do with its location. Not so. Key was originally *cayo* in Spanish, and simply meant an islet. The West part is even stranger. In Spanish, *huesco* means "bone," and when the Spaniards first got there they saw great quantities of unburied human bones. So *Cayo Huesco*—which became Key West—really meant the "Island of Bones"!

✳ Cathedrals take a long time to build. The Durham Cathedral in England was started in 1093. They were still working on it in 1500!

✳ When an area has tombs that go back more than 5,000 years, there are bound to be many bodies buried there. At Thatta, in Pakistan, near the ancient Mogul tombs, there is a section of six square miles that contains about 1 million graves!

✳ *Cuba* may sound like a Spanish name, but it isn't. The Lucayo, an indigenous people traveling with Columbus when he first saw the island, called it Cuba. Columbus first called it Juana, after the son of Ferdinand and Isabella. After Ferdinand's death it was called Ferdinandina. Later the name was changed to

Santiago, after St. James. Still later it was named Ana Maria, in honor of the Virgin Mary. And after all this, the only name that has survived is the original one, Cuba!

✳ In 1629, the emperor of India, Shah Jehan, went on a campaign to crush a rebellion in his kingdom. As always, his wife went with him on the long, arduous march. But she was ill and pregnant, and on the way she collapsed, gave birth to a daughter, and died. The empress was only 39 years old at that time, but the little girl was her fourteenth child.

The emperor was beside himself with grief. He carried his wife's body home, constantly wore the white robes of mourning, and went into seclusion.

Then one day, he appeared and gave orders that a beautiful palace was to be built for his wife. The body would lie there, he said, but it was never to be called a tomb. It was to be referred to by the Indian word *mahal*, meaning "palace"—and his wife was never to be spoken of as dead but as merely resting within her palace.

The palace that the emperor built for his beloved dead wife is one of the most breathtaking structures ever created by man . . . a dazzling wonder of marble and jewels known throughout the world today as the Taj Mahal.

✻ One of the most decisive battles in history, the Battle of Waterloo, was fought on June 18, 1815, by Napoleon Bonaparte against other European armies. Napoleon received his final defeat in the battle. However, in spite of its name, the battle was not fought in Waterloo itself but in a village in Belgium 2 miles to the south.

✳ If you want to see the spot where Christopher Columbus first set foot in the New World, don't look for elaborate monuments or statues. It is marked by a simple white cross set on a beach. And you can see it on the island of San Salvador in the Bahamas, a few miles from Cockburn Town.

✳ Near Füssun, in Bavaria, there stands Neuschwanstein Castle. It is so ornate and extravagant in design, it is impossible to believe that it made any sense to build it that way. Some experts believe that King Ludwig II of Bavaria, who had it built for him, wanted it designed that way because he was mentally ill!

✳ There is a lovely temple in Japan called the Silver Pavilion—but there isn't a touch of silver on it. It seems that the shogun (military ruler) who had it built as a country villa in 1479, intended to have the entire structure covered with silver. He just never got around to it.

❊ Death Valley, in Southern California, is probably the driest place in the Western Hemisphere. In 1850, a group of gold hunters and their families camped there for just one day. Less than half of them survived the heat and dryness! Ten years later, some prospectors came across the camp and saw the remains: wagons, chains, camp equipment, and children's toys. It's been known as Death Valley ever since.

❊ If you go to Troy, in Turkey, you can see nine different cities, one on top of the other! Archaeologists have uncovered these remains, and the seventh city is believed to be the Troy (Ilium) that Homer wrote about.

❊ Lots of people have a problem when it comes to spelling *Mississippi*. The name for that great river used to be much simpler. The Algonquins called it *Mechesebe*, meaning "Father of Waters." This was changed to

Michispe, then to *Misispi*, and finally by the explorer Marquette to *Mississippi*.

Mechesebe to Michispe to Misispi to Mississippi

❋ At Kandy, in Ceylon, there is a Temple of the Tooth, with a huge reclining statue of the Buddha, where one of the Buddha's teeth is preserved. And once every year, there is a religious festival there called the *Esala Perahera*, in which a jeweled casket with the tooth is carried in a dazzling procession day and night.

❋ Six hundred years ago, if you wanted to go to heaven when you died, you simply bought a certificate, called an indulgence, from the Catholic Church in Rome.

❇ The two great pyramids in Mexico are quite different from the Egyptian pyramids. The Pyramid of the Moon and the Pyramid of the Sun were not built as burial grounds but as temples of worship and astrological observatories. The Pyramid of the Sun is more than 200 feet high, and all the work was done by hand. What held the stones together? A mortar made of lime, sand, clay—and ground corn.

❇ The postal system used today started because an English poet was shocked by an old woman's trickery.

The poet was Samuel Taylor Coleridge, author of "The Rime of the Ancient Mariner," and the woman was a farmer's widow he met one day while taking a country walk.

Coleridge found the woman arguing with a postman about accepting delivery of a letter. At that time, all payments for postal services were based on distance, and the fee could be paid at either end. In this case, it was the woman who had to pay, but she had no money so the postman would not let her have the letter.

Touched by the woman's poverty, Coleridge paid the postage.

Instead of thanking him, however, the woman said he'd put out his money needlessly. The letter, she said, was from her son in the south of England. Every week he mailed her a blank piece of paper, and every week she refused to accept the mail. Her son had worked out this little trick so that his mother might know he was well without paying the high postage fee.

Coleridge was shocked. It seemed to him

that something was wrong with a system that made poor people resort to such trickery.

So Coleridge went to his friend Rowland Hill, then the postmaster general of England, and told him that the system must be reformed.

Hill agreed, and in 1839 the Penny Post Act became law. This act allowed an ordinary letter—prepaid by the first adhesive postage stamp ever used—to be sent anywhere in England for the same penny rate. This was the beginning of the world's modern postal system.

❋ It isn't often that a place gets named even before it's discovered. But this is actually what happened to a continent—Australia!

Australis means "southern" in Latin. When the mapmakers in the seventeenth century were studying the earth, they figured since there were all those great landmasses in the north, there had to be a great tract of land in the Southern Hemisphere to balance them. They marked this empty space *Terra Australis Incognita*—the Unknown Land of the South.

The Dutch, who got there first, called it New Holland. But in 1795, an English navigator, Matthew Flinders, called it Australia, meaning "south land,"—exactly what the mapmakers had called it before it was even discovered!

❋ In September 1944, Lieutenant Colonel Bertram Kalisch, an American pictorial officer stationed in Paris, received word from the public relations officer for the Ninth Army that something significant was about to happen in the vicinity of Romorantin, France. Kalisch picked up a film and sound crew and headed south to the area.

Kalisch learned that a Lieutenant Magill had made contact with German Major General Erich Elster and had bluffed him into believing that the Americans had a much larger force than they did. Magill's bluff worked well enough to have Elster consider surrender. An armed truce was set up while the Germans pondered the situation.

Kalisch took his film crew to Magill's headquarters, where they found a strange situation: This young American lieutenant was keeping a headquarters behind Germany lines with German orderlies. Kalisch, through a German staff officer, suggested to General Elster that, since he was considering surrender, he let Kalisch photograph a model German headquarters. Elster agreed. When the American photographer and the German general got together they discovered that Field Marshal Rommel, General Elster's commanding officer, and Kalisch's mother both came from Württemberg. The two officers became friendly immediately.

General Elster told Kalisch that he had not yet announced it to his troops, which numbered 20,000, but he was considering surrender. The American immediately told General Elster that such an historic event should be photographed. General Elster agreed to this, too. Kalisch, now promoting his unusual position for all its worth, reminded Elster of Cornwallis's surrender to Washington during the Revolution. He pointed out that a similar ceremony would be more fitting in the circumstances than the usual "table surrenders." Kalisch hastened to add that the German army would probably be reconstituted after the war and that Elster would probably face a board of inquiry. In facing a board of inquiry, Elster would want some photographs as proof that he surrendered his troops with honor—à la Cornwallis. General Elster was completely persuaded.

Kalisch selected a picturesque crossroads for the surrender scene. He convinced a Frenchman, who owned a house overlooking the area, that he should place his home at the disposal of the press for the historic occasion. All details arranged, General Magill and his staff—representing the American military, and Kalisch awaited Elster's arrival at the appointed hour. General Elster drove up in his staff car—late by a nervous 15 minutes—stepped out, saluted, and extended his apologies. He had a flat on the way. After Elster's personal surrender, 20,000 goose-stepping troops marched into the area from three different directions before the cameras. The films of this event were used worldwide and many copies were flown into Germany, where they did much to destroy morale there. Thanks to Lieutenant Colonel Kalisch, history had been recorded with the cooperation of everyone concerned—including the enemy.

❋ Men used to go to a barber-shop for more than just a haircut. Each shop had a red-and-white striped pole outside. This was because barbers used to "bleed" people. They cut a person's arm and let it bleed. This was thought to cure some illnesses. Barbers wrapped the used bandages around a pole and left them outside as an advertisement of their services.

✻ Vesuvius, 79 CE. That historic explosion
buried all of Pompeii under a hot, suffocating
blanket of ash and pumice 32 feet deep
and claimed the lives of more than 20,000
inhabitants. So quickly did the disaster take
place that only a few had time to escape. Most
victims died suddenly in their homes and
shops or as they fled toward the safety of the
nearby bay.

As the deadly sediment cooled, it hardened
around its victims, forming natural and perfect
molds of their bodies. Over the centuries, these

bodies gradually turned to dust, but the hard molds that outlined the once-living contours remained intact.

Almost 2,000 years later, workmen digging carefully down through the hard ash to unearth the ancient city would hear their tools tap on a hollow place. This sound told them that the body mold of a Pompeiian killed by Vesuvius lay beneath.

Upon this discovery, a hole would be carefully bored into the top of the "mold," and through this opening would be poured enough plaster of Paris to fill the empty space within. When the plaster hardened, the ancient covering would be broken away, revealing an absolutely lifelike case of one of Vesuvius's long-dead victims.

❉ Tourists who visit Warsaw are actually looking at a city that has been almost entirely rebuilt. The rebuilding was done using the original designs going back, in some cases, hundreds of years. During World War II, 90 percent of Warsaw was destroyed, and its population fell from 1,300,000 in 1939 to 162,000 in 1944.

✳ The great modern auction houses have had some strange items come under the hammer, but nothing as strange as that which went on the block in Rome in 193 CE. The bids taken at that auction were for possession of the Roman Empire, an area then covering several million square miles.

✳ The oldest surviving writing paper dates back to about 110 CE, and was made in China.

✳ Without an Englishman named Congreve, the United States would not have had its national anthem.

The rockets that inspired Francis Scott Key as he watched the bombardment of Fort McHenry on that historic night during the War of 1812 were the invention of Sir William Congreve, royal firemaster to the king. They were also the first rockets ever seen in America.

Made of narrow wooden tubes filled with gunpowder and tipped with iron warheads, the rockets were guided by simple, polelike rudders and launched from rows of tilted frames in a series of giant assaults. With a range of two miles, they were designed to explode on impact, scattering deadly shrapnel over a wide area.

Streaking across the sky, tails hissing and blazing, these new missiles were a terrifying sight. But they did not win the war for England. Instead, Congreve's rockets are remembered  today only because their brilliant "red glare" gave America its great "Star-Spangled Banner."

✳ Sometimes we feel that good bathrooms are a sign of the advance of modern civilization. At Knossos, on the island of Crete, there are ruins of a palace that was built about 4,000 years ago. It contains complete bathrooms with modern drainage systems!

✳ Gold certainly has a way of changing history. A gold rush will cause all kinds of people to settle in faraway places. And gold changed the whole history of Australia.

The British used to send convicts from their overflowing prisons to the American colonies. After the War of Independence, they had to find another place—and picked Australia.

Between 1788 and 1868, the British transported 155,000 convicts to Australia, which made it quite a penal colony. But in 1851 gold was discovered there, and that changed everything. The gold rush brought all kinds of "good people" from all over the world to Australia—and the new continent started a whole new life!

❉ The first escalator in Britain was put in Harrods department store in 1898. An attendant waited at the top and handed a glass of brandy to any customer who was upset by the ride.

❉ The only people in all of Europe who speak a Semitic language are the natives of the island of Malta. It is believed by some experts that Maltese is partly derived from the ancient dead language of the Phoenicians. But it is definitely a Semitic language, like Arabic and Hebrew.

✳ In the medieval city of Dinkelsbuhl in West Germany, a children's festival is held each July. It's not a festival to entertain children—but to thank them. It commemorates the role of children in saving the city from destruction during the Thirty Years' War, which was fought from 1618 to 1648.

✳ The Chinese used a shadow clock to tell the time more than 4,500 years ago.

✳ In 1903, a New England doctor named Nelson Jackson, who was on a vacation in San Francisco, made a bet that he could drive clear across the continent in the newfangled invention called the automobile.

A few days later, the daring doctor bought himself a 2-cylinder, 20-horsepower, chain-driven car and—with a companion—headed east on his pioneer journey.

The trip covered 6,000 miles and 11 states. The top speed attained was 20 miles per hour, and the roads were so bad that sometimes Jackson covered no more than 6 miles in a single day.

Frequently, he was stopped dead by breakdowns. Even minor repairs took days because tires had to come all the way from Akron, and spare parts from Cleveland.

Once, a farmer's wife purposely misdirected him so that her sister, who lived 50 miles away, would see a horseless carriage.

But the intrepid Jackson pushed on as fast as he could go and he finally made the East Coast. It took him 63 exhausting days and cost him $8,000 to win a $50 bet . . . but he was the first man in history to cross the United States by car.

✳ The Romans had no figure for zero. They used letters of the alphabet for the numbers 1, 5, 10, 50, 100, 500, and 1,000. This meant that they couldn't add columns of numbers.

Funny Laws/Lawsuits

Gainesville, Georgia, considers itself the "chicken capital of the world," and it's illegal there to eat chicken with a fork.

✳ In Newark, New Jersey, it's illegal to sell ice cream after 6 PM—unless the customer has a doctor's note.

❋ The state of Massachusetts forbids the eating of peanuts in church.

❋ In New Jersey, it is against the law to slurp soup.

❋ In Vermont, margarine cannot be served in a public eating place unless a notice is displayed saying that it is being offered.

❋ It was a tense moment in the bakery big leagues. The Pillsbury Doughboy, a television commercial star, was going head-to-head with Drox, the Hydrox cookie character, in a trademark infringement suit.

In spite of his giggles and excess weight, the Doughboy was a tough contender. Pillsbury had created him to market its rolls, and the Doughboy had been rising nicely to the occasion for more than 25 years. Drox was the brainchild of Sunshine Biscuits, Inc. The creamy little character came to life on TV from the filling of Hydrox cookies.

The two coexisted in peace until Drox got a facelift—and began looking a little too much like the Doughboy, according to Pillsbury. So Pillsbury filed suit (for an undisclosed amount of dough), and for a time it apeared that Drox and the Doughboy might actually slug it out in court.

But a last-minute settlement saved the day. Sunshine agreed to drop Drox (without admitting trademark infringement), and Pillsbury agreed to drop its suit.

✳ If you are sending a box of candy to your sweetheart in Idaho, it must weigh a minimum of 50 pounds.

✳ Nebraska tavern owners may not sell beer unless they are simultaneously brewing a kettle of soup.

✳ In Wisconsin, apple pie cannot be served without a cheese topping.

✳ In Boston, Massachusetts, legislators said a pickle should bounce four inches when dropped from waist height.

✻ If you are staying in California, do not peel an orange in your hotel room; it's illegal.

✻ Clarence worked in the kitchen of a cruise ship, filling ice-cream orders for the ship's waiters. He had scooped his way down to the middle of a 2.5-gallon tub one day when he reached a patch of ice cream that was "hard as a brickbat."

Clarence took an 18-inch butcher knife and was chipping away at the icy stuff when the knife slipped. He cut his hand—so badly that he lost two fingers. "Inadequate tools to safely perform the task." Clarence cried, and then proceeded to sue the shipping company.

A jury awarded Clarence $17,500, but the appeals court reversed the decision. Honestly now, who could have guessed that Clarence would use a butcher knife to chip the ice cream? the judge reasoned.

The case of the butchered ice cream made it all they way to the U.S. Supreme Court, which found in favor of Clarence after all. Someone should have transferred the ice cream out of the deep freeze earlier to soften it before serving, the Court ruled. Clarence shouldn't have been stuck with the "totally inadequate" scoop, and, yes, the employer *should* have foreseen that he "might be tempted to use a knife to perform his task with dispatch."

✲ In Columbus, Ohio, you can't legally sell corn flakes on Sunday.

❋ In Kansas, it is illegal for eateries to serve ice cream on cherry pie.

❋ When you're stuck with a giant metal tomato on the roof of your restaurant and you want to change your image, what do you do with the tomato? Pasquale's Restaurant came up with a great idea: Hold a contest and *award* it to somebody.

Alex and a bunch of his friends were dining out at Pasquale's. On a lark, Alex entered the contest to win the tomato by guessing its weight. He wrote "555 pounds" on a slip of paper, popped it in the slot, and forgot all about it.

So it came as a bit of a surprise some weeks later when Rich, the owner of Pasquale's, drove up to Alex's house with the giant tomato on a flatbed truck. It seems that Alex had come within 5 pounds of the exact weight. Since he didn't have space for the thing—it was 5 feet tall and 10 feet around—the two agreed to put it in storage.

The tomato made its way to the home of John, an employee of the restaurant. Before long, John began to stew. He claimed his employer owed him money for "expenses incurred" in storing the tomato.

Alex, meanwhile, was getting phone calls from people who actually wanted to buy the tomato. When one party offered $200, Alex agreed and he sent her to Rich, who sent her to John. The buyer got frustrated at this runaround, and Alex got mad. He filed suit against Rich. Rich filed suit against John.

Fed up, the judge ordered John to return the killer tomato to the restaurant. When the restaurant returned it to Alex, he dropped his suit—and promptly sold the tomato.

�֍ In Atlanta, it is against the law to secure a giraffe to a telephone pole or streetlamp.

✻ In Belvedere, California, an ordinance states: "No dog shall be in a public place without its master on a leash."

✻ In Texas, it's against the law to milk somebody else's cow.

✻ When Violet passed away, she left her $100,000 home to her beloved Skippy, a Pomeranian, to live in for the rest of his life. But this didn't set well with Violet's brothers and sisters. They went to court for permission to sell the house and divide the proceeds. "Sorry," said the judge, "you'll have to abide by the bequest and wait until Skippy's death."

Three years later, the silver-haired Skippy was still going strong at 13 years of age—about 90 in human terms—and Violet's heirs went to battle again. How can we be sure some other dog isn't being substituted? they wanted to know, and they demanded that Skippy have his leg tattooed.

That sounded pretty traumatic to Skippy's caretaker, a retired policeman who lived in the basement apartment in the dog's house. Skippy could be identified just as well through X-rays and photographs, he argued.

Once again, the judge found in favor of Skippy. The settlement did allow a detailed inspection of the dog's body to reassure the heirs.

❇ Platteville, Wisconsin: He filed for divorce after her plane trip. It seems she took out travel insurance and named their dog as beneficiary.

❄ In Galveston, Texas, it is against the law for camels to wander the streets unattended.

❄ In Brooklyn, New York, it is illegal for a donkey to sleep in a bathtub.

❄ Everybody knew that Nellie's pet geese had their nasty side. But Mike, Nellie's grandson, wasn't worried the day he dropped by for a visit. He was more concerned about Nellie herself, who was ailing.

When Mike stepped inside the fenced yard, however, the two geese and their three goslings saw red. They rushed at Mike, their necks outstretched. When he turned to run, he tripped and fell, cracking two fingers and a wrist.

When Mike got the doctor bills from his goose attack, it seemed only reasonable to send them to his grandmother's insurance company. No way! said the insurance company. You knew those geese were aggressive, and you assumed the risk when you walked in the gate.

Mike had only one option left: to sue his grandmother for $30,000. No hard feelings, he told Nellie, it's the insurance I'm after. In the end, he withdrew his suit, and grandma passed her geese along to a friend.

❋ If you're riding through Charleston, South Carolina, your horse better be wearing diapers.

❋ In California, it is against the law to detain a homing pigeon.

❋ In Massachusetts, all dogs must have their hind legs tied during the month of April.

❄ Do you remember the old joke "Why did the chicken cross the road?" Well, in Quitman, Georgia, it's illegal for a chicken to do so.

❄ In Lang, Kansas, it is against the law to drive down Main Street on a mule during the month of August unless your mule is wearing a straw hat.

❄ In Norfolk, Virginia, it is against the law for hens to lay eggs before 8 AM or after 4 PM.

✳ In New York City, you can go to jail if you open your umbrella in the presence of a horse.

✳ In the District of Columbia, it is illegal to fish on horseback.

✳ In the state of Vermont, it is illegal to whistle underwater.

✳ There is a law in Dunn, North Carolina, outlawing snoring and disturbing one's neighbors. The police can impose a two- or three-day jail sentence.

✳ In Los Angeles, California, you are forbidden to hunt moths under a streetlight.

✳ It is against the law in Louisiana to gargle in public.

✳ Bert Winkler, of Yazoo City, Mississippi, was brought to trial on charges of bank robbery. He convinced a friend to slip the jurors a note saying he'd give them each $1,000 if they acquitted him. After he was found not guilty, Winkler gave each juror $1,000, the judge $5,000, and the bailiff $250. He even gave $5 to each person who attended the trial, and gave the prosecuting attorney a nickel.

✳ A man in Eau Claire, Wisconsin, had promised a local medical group that he would one day donate his body for research. When the man had two teeth pulled, the medical group sued him because he did so without their permission.

❇ In the state of Washington, it's illegal to pretend that your parents are rich.

❇ Speaking English in the state of Illinois is illegal. In 1919, author H. L. Mencken had a statute revised establishing "American" as the official language.

❇ A woman in Norfolk, Nebraska, was brought to court for crossing the street against a red light. For this infraction she was fined $2.50. The woman gave the clerk a $5 bill and turned around to leave before receiving her change. When the judge called after her, she turned around and said: "That's okay, I need to cross back to the other side."

❇ In Pauling, Ohio, a police officer may bite a dog in an attempt to quiet him.

❇ In St. Louis, Missouri, it's illegal for an on-duty fireman to rescue a woman wearing a nightgown. If the woman wants to be rescued, she must be fully clothed.

✳ A local ordinance in Atwoodville, Connecticut, prohibits people from playing Scrabble while waiting for a politician to start speaking.

✳ If you live or work in Natoma, Kansas, it is in violation of the law to throw a knife at anyone wearing a striped suit.

✳ Domino players should be careful about playing the game in Alabama on Sundays. It's illegal.

✳ Winnemucca, Nevada: She snatched a letter from the postman that was in her husband's handwriting. When she opened the letter, she realized it was a love letter to another woman. She sued for divorce and won, but had to pay a fine of $20 for tampering with the mail.

✳ If you play hopscotch on the sidewalk in Missouri on Sunday, you will be in violation of the law.

✳ Point Charlotte, Florida: He filed for divorce immediately after they'd taken their vows. Why? Immediately after their I do's, she took him to her favorite bar and said to the bartender: "I told you I'd marry him. Now give me the $50."

✳ A 32-year-old woman in Rutland County, Vermont, was picked up for shoplifting in a supermarket. She had helped herself to $101.49 worth of batteries, cigarettes, doughnuts, and videotapes. The woman was charged with a felony, punishable by up to ten years in jail. Her public defender filed a motion asking the court to reduce the theft to a misdemeanor, which was punishable by a maximum of six months in jail. Apparently the threshold for a felony charge is $100 and the public defender claimed that the batteries and doughnuts were on sale, so the theft totaled only $97.37, just under the $100 threshold. The judge "bought it." The woman's charges were reduced to a misdemeanor.

✳ In the state of Nebraska, it's forbidden to sneeze in public. And in Omaha, it's illegal to burp or sneeze in church.

✳ In 1936, Denver, Colorado, passed a law stating that a dogcatcher must notify dogs of impounding by posting a notice for three con- secutive days on a tree in the city park and along a public road running through the park.

✳ At the Paiute Indian Reservation in California, a mother-in-law is prohibited from spending more than 30 days a year visiting her kids.

❉ You could go to jail in Georgia if you slap an old pal on the back.

❉ If a woman is in Bellingham, Washington, she is forbidden to take more than three steps backward while dancing.

❉ It's against the law for children under the age of seven to go to college in Winston-Salem, North Carolina.

❉ Although there are no *R* and *X* ratings for Ma Bell, in Blue Earth, Minnesota, it's against the law for children under 12 to talk on the telephone unless accompanied by a parent.

❉ In Iceland anybody can practice medicine, providing he/she hangs out a sign that reads SCOTTULAEJNIR, which means "quack doctor."

❋ It's against the law in Maine to walk down the street with your shoelaces untied.

❋ Nothing shady—but in Monroe, Utah, daylight must be visible between couples on a dance floor.

❋ Politicians in Preston, Idaho, aren't allowed to eat onions before speaking before a large group of voters within the city limits.

❋ It's illegal in Florida to doze off under a hair dryer.

❋ Another Florida law forbids a housewife from breaking more than three dishes a day.

❋ When Virginia saw what the *Gazette* had printed, she was so mad she could hardly see straight. There were profiles of all the candidates for the upcoming election, but the profile of *her* candidate, Kay, was garbled to the point where it made no sense.

"I don't think this was completely accidental," Virginia said to herself. "These guys were out to get my candidate!" So she wrote an angry letter to the editor of the *Gazette*. To make sure her letter would run in full, she asked that it be published as a paid ad and she sent the paper a check for $560. The *Gazette* printed Virginia's letter. Then it turned around and sued her for libel and slander.

"A man-bites-dog story!" said the appellate judge when the case reached his court. Nobody had ever heard of a newspaper suing over its own contents. A trial judge had ruled that this couldn't be done—but the *Gazette* appealed, on the grounds that Virginia had "compelled" it to print her ad.

Nobody compelled anybody, the appeals court found. The *Gazette* had freely chosen to publish Virginia's statements. And as the publisher, it couldn't sue, because "it is self-axiomatic that a person cannot sue himself or herself."

✳ If you happen to be on a shopping spree in Joliet, Illinois—beware. It's illegal for you to try on more than six dresses in any one store.

✳ It's illegal to sell suntan oil after noon on Sunday in Provincetown, Massachusetts.

✳ In the 1950s it was illegal for a flying saucer to land in the vineyards of France. It's now okay.

✻ In San Francisco, California, you'd better not get caught wiping your car with used underwear. It's unlawful.

✻ In California, a woman in a housecoat is forbidden to drive a car—and in Alabama you cannot drive a car while barefoot or in bedroom slippers.

✻ In Memphis, Tennessee, a woman cannot drive a car unless a man is running or walking in front of the car waving a flag to warn approaching pedestrians and motorists.

✻ In Roderfield, West Virginia, only babies are allowed to ride in baby carriages.

✻ A local ordinance in Brewton, Alabama, forbids the use of motorboats on city streets.

✻ In Glendale, Arizona, a car is forbidden to back up.

❋ Harold was driving his Chevy one winter day when suddenly he spotted another car coming at him in his own lane. He swerved, hit a chunk of ice, skidded into another chunk, and flipped his car—toppling 15 feet down into a gully with an icy stream at the bottom.

When he came to in his upside-down car, Harold saw lots of broken glass and twisted metal, but his own body parts seemed to be in working order. He was, however, in a jam. The car was wedged so tightly in the gully that he couldn't open either door, and the icy stream was gurgling past his ears.

Harold could hear cars passing above him, but blow the horn as hard as he might, he still couldn't make them hear him. He was starting to panic. Then Harold felt an enormous jolt. His car spun around in the creek, and when it stopped—bingo, he was able to open the door!

Sprung from his icy prison, Harold staggered out to see what had happened and discovered that—miraculously—a *second* car had crashed into the creek.

Did Harold fall on his knees and thank the driver, Lucas, for saving his neck? Hardly. Pointing to the back injury he had gotten when the two cars collided, he sued Lucas for $10,000.

A trial judge scoffed at this suit. There wasn't a shred of evidence that Lucas was negligent, he said.

But when Harold appealed his case, he had better luck. Harold had a *right* to be in that creek, said the appeals court judge. He proved he got there through no fault of his own, forced off the road by an oncoming driver.

And once he was there, he had a right to peace and quiet.

But what right did Lucas have accidentally landing on top of Harold? Lucas, said the judge, hadn't *proved* he had any more business in the creek than "in a cornfield or in somebody else's front yard."

✳ If you're a motorist passing through Pennsylvania and sight a team of horses coming toward you, you must pull well off the road, cover your car with a blanket or canvas that blends in with the countryside, and let the horses pass. If one of the horses is skittish, you must take your car apart piece by piece and hide it under the nearest bush.

✳ In Omaha, Nebraska, each driver on a country road is required to send up a skyrocket every 150 yards, wait 8 minutes for the road to clear, and then drive cautiously, blowing the horn while shooting off a Roman candle.

❋ It's a crime punishable by death to put salt on a railroad track in Alabama.

❋ There's a law in Maine that prohibits anyone from stepping out of a plane while it's in the air.

❋ The legislature in the state of Kansas passed a law stating: "When two trains approach each other at a crossing, both shall come to a full stop and neither shall start up again until the other has gone."

❋ In Minneapolis, Minnesota, anyone who double-parks an auto shall be put on a chain gang and fed bread and water.

❋ When a car struck and damaged his "beautiful oak tree," a man named Elsworth was so dismayed that he took the owner of the car and the woman who was driving it to court. He also wanted a judgment against the insurance company covering the vehicle.

Elsworth got nowhere with the trial court. The owner and driver were immune from liability thanks to the state's no-fault insurance act, and the insurance company couldn't be dragged in because Elsworth hadn't gotten the procedure right.

So Elsworth appealed his case. Though the verdict was no different, he did inspire Judge J. H. Gillis of Michigan to write a poetic opinion on behalf of the three-justice panel:

We thought that we would never see
A suit to compensate a tree
A suit whose claim in tort is prest
Upon a mangled tree's behest;
A tree whose battered trunk was prest
Against a Chevy's crumpled crest;
A tree that faces each new day
With bark and limb in disarray;
A tree that may forever bear
A lasting need for tender care.
Flora lovers though we three,
We must uphold the court's decree.

❋ Susanville, California: She sued him for divorce because he sold the kitchen stove in order to get the money to purchase liquor to feed his habit. He owned up to the fact that he did sell the stove, but he begged the court for leniency because she didn't miss the stove for two weeks.

✳ In Milwaukee, Wisconsin, a motorist cannot park an auto for more than two hours unless it is hitched to a horse.

✳ Parviz Mahin, a janitor at a bus depot in Ankara, Turkey, found a bag of precious stones worth $7.3 million. A Good Samaritan, he returned the stones to the jeweler. The jeweler didn't offer any reward. Mr. Mahin asked the jeweler for a small diamond ring for his wife. The jeweler refused, and Mr. Mahin took the ring. The jeweler pressed charges and Mr. Mahin had to spend six years in jail.

✳ In Kankakee, Illinois, a woman brought charges against a man because he called her a chicken. The judge asked the woman how much she weighed, calculated what she would cost per pound if she were a chicken, and fixed that sum as the fine.

❊ Marshfield, Wisconsin: When the couple married, he promised to pay her $1 for each kiss as long as they remained married. She sued him for divorce and asked the court for an award of $3,000 in back payments.

❊ In Virginia it's illegal to take a bath in a tub if the tub is located in any room attached to the house.

✳ In Oklahoma there was a legendary legislator named "Alfalfa Bill" Murray. He was a rather tall chap and was continually irked when he went into hotels and found the bed linens too short to cover his long, lanky body. So in 1908 he had a law passed requiring all hotels to have nine-foot sheets.

✳ You can file suit against the Devil himself and have your day in court, Adolph found, but you won't necessarily get any satisfaction. Adolph filed a civil rights action against "Satan and his staff." The defendant, he claimed, had "on numerous occasions caused him misery" and had "placed deliberate obstacles in his path and caused his downfall."

That might well be, said the judge, but there wasn't anything he could do about it. First, he noted, "we question whether Adolph may obtain personal jurisdiction over the defendant in this judicial district." Nobody knew for sure whether Satan had his legal residence there.

The case might be considered as a class action, the judge went on, but that was going to be tough given the vast size of the "class"— and the question of whether Adolph's claims were representative of everyone else's. Finally, the judge noted, Adolph hadn't given any instructions as to exactly how the U.S. marshal was supposed to serve process on Satan and his servants.

In this case, at least, the Devil came out "not guilty."

❋ As the salutatorian of her high school class, Shelly took her grade-point average seriously— very seriously. One day she missed algebra class. Since she had no excuse, the teacher lowered her grade—and that meant a slip in her overall grade-point average from 95.478 to 95.413.

Now .065 might not sound like much; but to Shelly's dad, Ralph, you start letting the little things go and pretty soon the big ones will follow. Ralph saw only one solution: to sue the school board for a million dollars.

That docked grade point was a violation of his daughter's Fifth and Fourteenth Amendment rights, Ralph told the court. The judge consented to the reinstatement of the grade points, but he refused to award any money. Ralph appealed the decision, hoping at least to get his attorney's fees paid—but the appeals court judge was so exasperated he took the grade points away again. "Patently insubstantial" was how the judge saw this case.

✳ In Baton Rouge, Louisiana, the state house of representatives passed a law stating that maximum of 25 cents can be charged to cut the hair of bald men.

✳ In Nogales, Arizona, they "let it all hang out": It is illegal to wear suspenders.

✳ A law in Boston, Massachusetts, has rendered it illegal to bathe without a written prescription from a doctor.

✳ In Lake Charles, Louisiana, there is a law making it illegal for a rain puddle to remain on your front lawn for more than 12 hours.

✳ Two attorneys in Hartford, Connecticut, wrote their own wedding vows. The vows of Bernard Prothroe and Annamarie Kendall covered 47 single-spaced, 8½ x 14-inch, type-written pages. It took the officiator more than five hours to read them. By the time the ceremony was over, 90 percent of the guests had left—including the parents of the bride and groom.

✳ "Cole Porter has been swiping my tunes for just about long enough," Lenny decided—and he sued the famous songwriter for copyright infringement. It wasn't Lenny's first lawsuit, not by a long shot. Over the years, he'd sued five other composers for the same offense.

Cole Porter hadn't dreamed up "My Heart Belongs to Daddy" all by himself, Lenny claimed. The tune came from Lenny's "A Mother's Prayer." "Begin the Beguine" came from there, too. "Night and Day" was stolen from Lenny's "I Love You Madly," and "Don't Fence Me In" was right out of "A Modern Messiah."

Lenny wanted "at least $1 million out of the millions Cole Porter is earning out of all the plagiarism." When the judge asked Lenny where Porter might have heard his music in order to copy from it, Lenny pointed out that "A Mother's Prayer" had sold more than a million copies. As for the other pieces, most of them had been played at least once over the radio.

Besides, Lenny claimed, Cole Porter "had stooges right along to follow me, watch me, and live in the same apartment with me." His room had been ransacked several times, he said.

"How do you know Cole Porter had anything to do with it?" the judge asked. "I don't know that he had anything to do with it; I only know that he *could* have," Lenny explained.

The district judge found Lenny's whole story fantastic and dismissed it. The appeals court, though, did find similarities between Lenny's music and Cole Porter's. Yes, the judge admitted, that part about the stooges was pretty weird, but "sometimes truth is stranger than fiction." It would be up to a jury to decide.

Sadly for Lenny, the jury didn't swallow his story. He appealed again—he even petitioned the U.S. Supreme Court—but finally he had to compose himself and go home.

❄ A man and woman were dining at a restaurant in Scranton, Pennsylvania. The woman ordered an oyster dish. The oyster contained a pearl that was valued at $750. Both the woman and the restaurant owner claimed they owned the pearl, and the case went to court. The judge, in his attempt to make an impartial ruling, awarded the pearl to the gentleman who paid for the woman's dinner.

✳ In Mahdia, Tunisia, a 67-year-old philanthropist died, leaving his worldly goods to his wife, 9 children, 13 grandchildren, aunts, uncles, nieces, nephews, friends, business associates, mailman, and secretary. He didn't, however, include his gardener or his barber. They've contested the will. The case is pending, and so far no one's collected a cent.

✳ Drugstores in Providence, Rhode Island, may sell toothbrushes on Sunday—but not toothpaste.

✳ A Minnesota tax form asked for all sorts of information. It requested that you fill in your date of birth and your date of death.

Mixed Bag

When people say "Rome," they usually mean the capital of Italy. But there are cities called Rome on every continent! In the United States, there are Romes in New York, Virginia, Iowa, Kansas, Texas, Pennsylvania, Indiana, and Georgia. And there are two Romes in Argentina!

✳ During the Middle Ages, from about 1000 CE onward, the peasants of northern Europe wore carved wooden shoes called sabots. These shoes were identical to present-day Dutch wooden shoes.

Interestingly, the word *sabotage* comes from *sabot.* When a peasant wished to avenge himself on his landlord, he trampled the landlord's crops with his sabots. Sabotage today means to destroy deliberately.

❋ A hotel in San Juan, Puerto Rico, is shaped like a huge ship. Appropriately, it's called the Normandie—after the French liner that inspired the design of the hotel.

❋ The fossil bones of certain ancient reptiles were dug up in North Yorkshire, England. The local residents there call them fallen angels. They believe these bones belonged to angels who were cast out of heaven for having rebelled.

❋ For a certain estate in Yorkshire, England, the tenant has been paying the same rent for hundreds of years. It is a red rose at Christmas and a snowball at Midsummer. The original landlord felt this would make it very hard to pay the rent. But the tenant doesn't mind. He grows roses under glass, and he collects snow from the moor on the estate. Sometimes, however, the snowball is about the size of a pea!

✳ All varieties of domestic canaries are descendants of the wild canary. The wild canary is a native of Madeira, the Azores, and the Canary Islands. Although the canary bird is in fact named after the Canary Islands, the islands themselves owe their name to another animal.

The Romans called the islands *Insulae Canariae,* which means "islands of the dogs." The Romans gave the islands the name because so many canines lived there. The Canary Islands, therefore, are not named after birds but after dogs.

✳ Ancient Egyptian women painted black eye makeup around their eyes. This helped to reduce the glare of the sun.

✳ Pilgrims who visit St. Patrick's Purgatory, a tiny island on a lake in Donegal, Ireland, have to observe certain strict rules. These include fasting on dry bread and black tea, and going barefoot all day.

✳ The Torah, which consists of the Five Books of Moses, the first five books of the Bible, is found in every Jewish synagogue. But every single Torah is prepared in a very special way. A Torah must be written by hand, with a feather pen, and on a special kind of parchment.

✳ What father had the most children? Well, in the Western world the palm must go to Niccolo III, who ruled the independent Italian city of Ferrara from 1393 to 1441. During his long reign, through a succession of wives and mistresses that shocked even his free-and-easy age, he fathered almost 300 children.

❋ When a politician campaigns for office, he tries to make people think he is "one of them." In the continental United States, it might mean eating certain foods or wearing certain hats. But in Hawaii, no politician dares run for office without knowing how to do the hula! It's part of the campaign.

❋ The Swiss guards, the personal bodyguards of the Pope, are really Swiss. They are recruited in the Catholic cantons of Switzerland. The reason they wear those particular uniforms is that the treaty that established the guard was signed in the sixteenth century—and that's the uniform they wore in those days!

✳ Many years ago, a village priest in the little town of Zipaquira, Colombia, dreamed of someday having a beautiful church for his little flock, all of whom were poor workers in the local salt mine. The mine there is the largest active salt mine in the world, and it supports the entire town.

The priest's dream came true. But the church grew into a cathedral—and it is made entirely of salt!

The cathedral, called Our Lady of the Rosary, is constructed entirely within a towering mountain of salt, 800 feet beneath the summit. Everything within the cathedral is carved and shaped from the hard, glistening white salt: the towering pillars, the great vaulted dome, the Stations of the Cross, the side chapels, the statuary, the magnificent central altar. And all the work of construction, of carving and shaping, was done by the devout miners.

The cathedral took 6 years to build, and can seat 5,000 worshipers. The great nave is 400 feet long, 73 feet high, and is supported by columns of solid salt 33 feet square. The workmen who built it used pneumatic drills in constructing it.

Our Lady of the Rosary is reached by way of deep tunnels, each a mile long, and wide enough for the passage of a single car; one tunnel leads in, the other winds out. Just outside the gates to this strange house of worship is a vast underground parking lot that has enough space to accommodate more than 200 cars.

✳ About a hundred years ago in India, Sikhs used a Frisbee-like weapon. They twirled a razor-sharp metal quoit on one finger and hurled it at the enemy.

✻ St. Pantaleone was once the patron saint of Venice, Italy. He was later depicted in a play as a silly old man who wore long trousers. From the play, trousers were called pantaloons, later shortened to *pants.*

✻ The Poets' Corner in Westminster Abbey, in London, England, contains the remains of many great writers and poets. This includes the ashes of Thomas Hardy. But his heart is not there. It is buried in a grave at Stinsford, in Dorset.

❊ A temple to Kuan Yin, the goddess of mercy, was built in Hong Kong for a very unusual reason. About 50 years ago, workers were digging a well when suddenly a geyser erupted. It had crimson water because of deposits of mercury and sulfur there. But the diggers thought they had wounded a sacred dragon and it was the dragon's blood that they saw—so they built a temple on that site.

❊ At approximately 146,000 square miles, the total area of Japan is slightly smaller than the state of Montana. It is a chain of islands that has a north-to-south span of about 1,300 miles. This is such a long distance that the vegetation is completely different at each end of the country.

❊ The Pygmies happen to be the smallest humans on earth, averaging 4 feet 11 inches, but the effect of their favorite arrow poison is anything but diminutive. Derived from the formidable red ant, it is so poisonous that a single poisoned arrow will fell a full-grown elephant.

✻ There were no sparrows or starlings in North America until about a hundred years ago, when a New Yorker imported the birds. He wanted the United States to have all the birds named in Shakespeare's plays.

✻ If you see a clock with Roman numerals, is 4 expressed as *IV*? It should be, but usually it's done by four strokes, *IIII*. There is an odd reason for this. When Louis XIV would look at his watch, he always confused the IV and the VI. So he sent it back to the watchmaker to make the change. And, of course, everybody copied the king's example. We still do!

✳ Kulang, China, runs seven centers for recycled toothpicks. People rummage through garbage cans to find toothpicks. They wash them, check for splinters, and are paid the equivalent of 35 cents a pound for reusable toothpicks.

✳ When you watch the Mehter band of the Turkish army on parade, their costumes will seem strange. That's because they're styled after those worn by soldiers during the sixteenth century. The Mehter band happens to be the oldest military band in the world.

✳ Sailing enthusiasts wishing to explore the Great Sound off Bermuda find they must pass through Somerset Bridge, which joins

Somerset Island to the mainland. Passersby are always willing to lend a helping hand as they steer the mast of your boat through the narrow 18-inch opening and then replace the center board of the bridge so that waiting traffic can be on its way.

✳ Democracy in a very direct form is still practiced in many communes in Switzerland. An open-air *Landsgemeinde* ("citizens' assembly") is held on the public square, and all the people decide by a show of hands which laws are to be enacted.

✳ It is popularly assumed that the human shape of scarecrows is what frightens off crows and other birds. However, it is not the resemblance to the shape of humans that scares the

birds, but the smell. The scent of humans on the scarecrow's clothing is what frightens the birds. After exposure to wind and rain, the clothing of the scarecrow loses its human smell and with it, its effectiveness. A scarecrow that has been out in the open for any length of time may provide a decorative touch in your garden or field, but it will not rid you of crows or other birds.

❋ Man can live practically anywhere he chooses on earth, but he can't always build up a community in faraway places. Where is the northernmost spot on earth he has managed to establish a town?

It's near the top end of Norway, called Hammerfest, and it's a nice little town with all the comforts of home—plus a few unusual ones.

For one thing, the people in this town see sunshine around the clock from May 13 to July 29. But it's very quiet and dark—no sun at all!—from November 18 to January 23.

The temperature? Surprisingly enough, in January the average temperature in Hammerfest is just a little below the freezing point!

✳ South American Indians use the chemical called bufotenine (from the skins of poisonous toads). It is also employed in their cohoba snuff (*Piptadenia peregrine*) to promote a feeling of well-being when they hold dances. In larger doses, cohoba induces trances during which the Indians speak with their gods and the spirits of their dead.

✳ There are only about 1,200 people in Ushuaia, Argentina. But this makes it a "town." And so the natives of Ushuaia, which is at the very bottom of the southern tip of Argentina, claim that theirs is the southernmost town in the world. They say that the few communities that are farther south have so few people they are mere hamlets.

✳ Foretelling the future is becoming a popular—and highly paid—business. But few sooth-sayers will ever be able to equal the record of Jules Verne in predicting what's ahead for the world.

First and foremost among all science-fiction writers, Verne reached the peak of his writing career before the start of the twentieth century. In his books, he prophesied atomic submarines, the military tank, skyscrapers, aircraft, television, earth-moving machines, talking pictures, and a host of other modern inventions. And not only did he predict them, he explained how they would work.

But Verne's most uncanny forecast of things to come was his detailed description of a voyage to the moon. Verne described a moon rocket long before anyone dreamed of such a thing, and even told of a dog that would be sent up first—as the Russians did—to test the projectile.

Most amazing of all, however, in his book *Round the Moon*, this fantastic man actually described the place from which a moon rocket would take off. These are his words:

"Everyone in America made it his duty to study the geography of Florida. As a point of departure for the moon rocket, they had chosen an area situated 27 degrees North Latitude and 5 degrees West Longitude."

That location is only 80 miles from Cape Kennedy.

✳ In Hialeah, Florida, a woman was admitted to the local hospital for abdominal pains. After coming up with baffling results to all their standard diagnostic tests, the doctors finally found that the patient was infested with termites.

✳ The strangest task ever performed by monkeys was undertaken during the nineteenth century, in Africa. European visitors, returning from Ethiopia at that time, brought back the exotic news that monkeys were used as torch-bearers during royal feasts. The animals were trained to sit absolutely motionless, lighting the scene, until after the guests had finished eating. Then the monkeys were rewarded by being allowed to finish off what was left of the sumptuous meal.

✳ A tax collector named Louis Dobermann lived in Germany about 120 years ago. He was not welcome when he came to collect money. To protect him, he bred large, fierce dogs. They became known as Doberman pinschers, and are still used as guard dogs today.

✳ Franz Joseph Haydn, the great Austrian composer, died in 1809 and was buried in an old Vienna cemetery.

One night, shortly after his burial, two men opened the grave and severed Haydn's head from his body. They did this in the belief that an examination of the master's skull would disclose the secret of his genius. It did not, but one of the men kept the head until his own death in 1839. Then the grave robber's widow, anxious to get rid of her ghastly treasure, turned the head over to a family friend who was a doctor.

The doctor kept the head for 13 years, then gave it to a professor who was the director of the famous Vienna Pathological Institute.

Eventually the professor died and by his will Haydn's head was given to the Vienna Society of the Friends of Music.

About this time, the public became aware of the pitiful progress of Haydn's head. There was then a great public outcry and, at the insistent demand of the people, the head was transferred for the last time. On June 5, 1954, there was a new burial ceremony and the head of the great musical genius, Joseph Haydn, was finally reunited with his body, thus ending a posthumous journey of almost 145 years.

✳ In South America there is a tribe of people called the Mocoui, among whom it is considered very important for the men to be able to run fast. It helps in the hunt. So the men of the Mocoui tribe tie deer hooves to their wrists and ankles, believing this will make them "swift as the deer."

✳ Some time ago, Ichimonji, a popular pet donkey at the big Tokyo Zoo, fell prey to the ravages of his 29 years and lost all his teeth. Visiting tots, arriving at the zoo with bundles of juicy carrots, wept at the sight of their ancient little friend who could no longer chew their vegetable offerings.

Touched by this, the zoo authorities called upon the Tokyo Medical School to do something about the situation. Their plea was answered.

Doctors and students alike contributed generously and, providing Ichimonji with a $2,000 set of gold-filled false teeth, they fully restored the shaggy little pet his former capacity for carrot munching.

✳ The straw hat known as the Panama does not come from Panama. The hat actually comes from Ecuador.

❋ The first recorded use of toothpaste was about a thousand years ago by a Roman named Scribonius Largus. It was a mixture of honey, salt, and ground glass. Ancient Spaniards dipped their toothbrushes in human urine.

❋ The huge Swiss alpenhorn was originally used as a call to battle or a warning of fire in the high mountain districts of Switzerland. And no wonder: When a Swiss blows into the horn, and the wind is right, it can be heard eight miles away!

✻ Pigs certainly seem harmless enough, but a pig in Lüneburg, Germany—acting undoubtedly in self-defense—shot a butcher who was just about to dispatch the animal with a pistol. The man, kneeling beside the pig to load his gun, suddenly found himself the victim of his own bullet when a porcine hoof kicked up and hit the trigger.

✻ One of Hawaii's many ornamental plants is the castor bean (*Ricinus communis*). At times it grows into a large tree, the seeds of which are processed for the castor oil they contain. But in their raw, unprocessed condition, the seeds of this tree contain a powerful poison called ricin. The seeds themselves could be swallowed whole with no effect, but if as little as 1/100 of a milligram of ricin gets into the blood it becomes a fatal dose. Ricin clumps together red blood cells and causes internal bleeding on the inside as well as severe kidney damage and other dangerous effects.

❊ Pisa isn't the only place in the world with a leaning tower. Glamorgan, Wales, has one, too: Caerphilly Castle, built by the Normans.

❊ We think of people who curse as having bad manners. But is cursing somebody really nothing more than that?

We know that many cultures have a great fear of magic words. These are used in ceremonies for injuring or destroying their enemies. And it was the ancient use of magic words against others in order to get vengeance or do them harm that led to the custom of cursing. So watch your language!

❊ The lei is practically a symbol of Hawaii. To put one together takes considerable skill and hard work. In a single necklace there may be as many as 450 blossoms, and the individual flowers are shaped and formed into strings by hand.

❋ The way the dashboard of an automobile looks is no accident. It was carefully planned and designed, as are all the parts of the car. And one of the most important people in deciding the best arrangement for the series of dials or buttons is a psychologist! "Engineering psychologists" are used by industry to help in designing products and machines because they understand human reactions.

❋ Being called a whistle punk doesn't sound very flattering. But that's the name for the man who gives the signals to the other crew members in a lumberjack gang. The men are divided into sides, and each whistle punk is responsible for all the signals to his side.

❋ Where are we heading? Don't ask this of a Swedish sailor if you happen to be on his ship.

Swedish sailors think it's bad luck to mention the name of the port for which they are bound.

✳ You can speak English—but can you also speak Egyptian? Probably not. But a surprising thing about the two languages is that many English and Egyptian words are very similar!

These two languages belong to completely different "families," but here are some almost identical words with similar meanings from each:

ENGLISH	EGYPTIAN
abode	abut
attack	atakh
nature	natr
twist	tust
youth	uth

And there are many, many others! Nobody knows whether it's coincidence, or whether they were related in some way long ago.

✳ Tourists who try to photograph picturesque natives in remote parts of Mexico run into trouble. There are people there who believe that the camera catches and keeps their souls.

✳ The expression "It's a white elephant" is used when people want to say that something costs more to maintain or operate than it's worth. It comes from what a certain king of Siam is supposed to have done. He used to make a present of a white elephant to members of his court whom he wanted to ruin, knowing they couldn't afford to keep the white elephant in the proper style.

But there's more behind the white elephant than that. In Siam, even today, it is believed that a white elephant contains the soul of a dead person, maybe even an ancient god. So when a white elephant is captured, it is cared for and worshipped. And when a white elephant dies, it is mourned for like a human.

✾ A Persian wheel is an ancient way of raising water from a well. To turn the wheel, a blindfolded camel or bull walks around in a circle. It may be an ancient device, but in Pakistan today, there are still 200,000 Persian wheels in operation!

✾ Fashions have strange ways of getting started and then being copied—but can you imagine a law that decided the shape of the handkerchief you now use?

It actually happened in France. Marie Antoinette didn't like having handkerchiefs made in all sizes and shapes. Some were oblong, some round, some triangular, and some square. She felt that the square form was the most convenient for a handkerchief, and they should only be made that way.

So she asked Louis XVI to issue a law, and on June 2, 1785, the king decreed that "The length of hand-kerchiefs shall equal their width, throughout my entire kingdom." Handkerchiefs have remained square ever since!

✳ The human bone seems to be quite strong and able to last a very long time. Sometimes it is even used for architecture or wall decoration.

If you want to see walls and pillars lined with human bones, go to the monastery of St. Francis in Évora, Portugal, about 70 miles from Lisbon.

In 712, Évora was conquered by the Moors, and it remained under Moorish domination until 1166. In a chapel of the church of the monastery, the walls and pillars are covered with human skulls and bones!

❊ Gypsies may roam about a great deal, but they also get together on certain occasions. On May 25 every year, Gypsies from all over Europe meet at the town of Saintes-Maries de la Mer in France. They carry a statue of Sarah into the Mediterranean in a ritual procession. This is to honor Sarah, who they believe to be their ancestress, and who is supposed to be buried there.

❊ The Mr. Yuk label was used for many years as an effective safety measure to protect small children. The biggest reason for its effectiveness was that it was designed by children and for children, with a good steering committee of mothers and teachers. The objective was to find an image that a child under five years old could easily identify with and instantly recognize as a no-no.

The old skull and crossbones was rejected because it has lost its meaning, for it has become a cultural icon. To get to the heart of the matter, young children were asked what they though of when they heard the word *poison*. They replied that poison can kill, it makes you sick, and mothers yell if you play with it. Researchers realized that children are hard to scare—witness their delight in horror movies. They seem to be unshakable. But the tests showed that there was one sensation that repulsed them all—throwing up. This is what the picture of Mr. Yuk reminds them of. This and the ghastly green color made the perfect turnoff signal. (The name, incidentally, is said to have come from a little boy who said it looked "yukky.") The Mr. Yuk label was officially retired in 2003.

❋ The Highland Light in Truro, Massachusetts, is so powerful that it can be seen from a ship 20 miles away at sea.

❋ The painter Vincent van Gogh was named after a brother who had died at birth. All Vincent's life, there was a grave with his name on it.

❋ You can't stop a tourist from taking pictures of unusual things he sees on his trip. And there is hardly a tourist with a camera who has come to a certain railway station in Norway and not taken its picture.

The reason is obvious. And the jokes that result from it must be rather tiresome. It's because the name of this railroad station is Hell.

✻ Next time you see a man wearing a hat, notice the band around it. There is absolutely no need for this band—yet hats are not made without them.

It's a curious remnant of a truly ancient custom. The Egyptians used to wear a band around the head to keep their hair in place when traveling. But in time, hats began to be worn. People still wanted to have that band—so it was put around the hat. And the hatband is still with us today!

✳ A street in Guanajuato, Mexico, is so narrow that it is called "the Street of the Kiss." That's because sweethearts can kiss each other from their opposite balconies!

✳ The largest Mormon temple west of Salt Lake City, Utah, is in Laie—a suburb of Honolulu, Hawaii

✳ In 1865, an American woman named Mary Mapes Dodge wrote a children's classic called *Hans Brinker or the Silver Skates*. From this book, generations of Americans have grown up familiar with the story of the heroic little Dutch boy who, by putting his finger in the dike, saved his native city of Haarlem from being flooded.

Many of these Americans traveled to Holland to visit the ancient city on the North Sea Coast and find the place where little Hans had held the dike. But in Haarlem they would be told the sad truth that Hans Brinker had lived only in the imagination of the author and that the Dutch had never even heard of him. He was purely an American legend.

But the legend persisted despite the facts; Americans would *not* let it die. They just kept turning up asking about Hans Brinker.

So the good people of Holland decided to do something about the matter.

Today, on the outskirts of Haarlem, you may see the delightful statue of a little boy holding his finger in a leaking dike. The statue bears the name and form of Hans Brinker, the mythical boy, but the Dutch have erected it to honor all the brave men and women who have worked—and died—to keep the dikes of Holland strong.

✳ In the United States, a popular rhyme about the health benefits of the apple goes like this: "An apple a day keeps

the doctor away." In England, they express the same idea this way: "Eat an apple going to bed; make the doctor beg his bread."

✻ In the Cambodian hamlet of Paoy Pet, children outnumber adults five to one. The voting age is seven, and the mayor is only nine. Because children rule, they can punish their parents if they've been bad.

✻ A dog can hear a range of sounds—from quiet to loud—two and a half times greater than that heard by humans. A human can make a range of sounds nearly twice as great.

✻ The worship of stones is a very ancient and widespread stage in the development of religion. This is probably because ancient people believed that when a person died, his or her spirit entered the stone and lived there. For example, in parts of Central America, when an important man died, a stone was put into his mouth to receive his soul.

Are stones still being worshipped today? Among some people in India and China, yes. And among Native Americans, the Pueblos believe that when they go hunting, their success depends entirely on the stones they carry with them.

✳ In West Africa there are several tribes that use poisons both for hunting and to preserve tribal law and order by the "ordeal of poison." They use a poison called *mauvi* in their trial-by-ordeal rituals. *Mauvi* is made by scraping the bark from certain tree—known only to the witch doctor—and mixing it with water.

The rites of the ordeal are very specific. The brew is given to both the accused and his accuser. The natives believe that the guilty one will die. If the brew is good, death will be quick: vomiting, convulsions, then death—rapidly and in that order. If it turns out that both parties merely throw up and live, then the brew is declared badly prepared and the contest is, temporarily, a draw—temporarily because a new brew is prepared and the contest continues until death actually points its ghastly finger at the wrongdoer. When death does finally occur, the guilty one's wife and children are also put to death. All terms of the tribal contract are carried out and overseen by a highly rewarded tribal official who must also pay the brewer's fee. The natives believe this test is infallible, and submit to it eagerly to prove their innocence if they are ever accused of evil deeds.

✻ What are the safest years in the life of a person in the United States? The chances of surviving from one year to the next are greatest at the ages of 9, 10, and 11. The mortality rate is the lowest during these years.

9 ^{10} 11

✳ The master–slave manipulator has nothing to do with masters or slaves. It's a pair of artificial hands, with forearms, wrists, fingers, and thumbs, used by research workers who deal with radioactive substances. The research worker, safe behind a window of lead glass, can make the master–slave manipulator do anything he could possibly do with his own hands!

✳ The *nuraghi* are some of the strangest monuments in the world. Built by people who invaded the island of Sardinia about 5,000 years ago, nuraghi are made of rough, unhewn stones piled up to form a round tower with walls that slope inward. There were once about 8,000 of these towers, and there are now about 6,500 left. And nobody is sure why they were ever built in the first place.

✳ It's amusing, most people who see it smile, and it's considered practically a trademark of the city. It's the *Manneken-Pis*, the statue of the little boy "urinating" into the fountain near the Grande Place in Brussels, Belgium.

But the Belgians don't just look at the Manneken. Whenever there is some special occasion that calls for it, they dress the popular little statue in a costume. He is said to have a very large wardrobe that includes everything from Boy Scout uniforms to native dress from many parts of the globe!

❋ He is called *Goliathus goliathus*, which is like saying "giant giant." But the name fits him well, since this monster beetle from Africa is the biggest bug in the world. Stretched out, he measures six inches or more in length and has a wingspan of eight inches.

The only living Goliath beetle ever known to be in the United States was seen several years ago at New York's Museum of Natural History.

Affectionately called Buster the Bug by an admiring staff, the Goliath had been secretly left one Christmas Eve on the museum's doorstep. He was found inside a covered coffee can lined with grass—obviously an effort made to protect him from the wintry blasts.

Buster was installed in a fine, temperature-controlled glass house and fed a lush diet of ripe melons, mangoes and tomatoes. He gained weight (almost half an ounce) and seemed happy to do nothing else but loll around as the museum's star attraction.

Only one sticky little incident marred the idyll of this *coleopteron* (the scientific name for beetles). That was when Buster's fame spread to the immigration department. The department, which takes a very dim view of any insect being imported into the United States, promptly declared Buster an undesirable alien and ordered his demise. But Dr. John C. Pallister, chief entomologist at the museum, would have none of that, and went to bat for his rare bug.

It is very hard for anyone to win an argument with a scientist. So in the end Buster was allowed to stay on at the museum. He was given a special "passport," and Dr. Pallister promised that "adequate safeguard measures would be employed to prevent escape."

✳ Waves wear away the coasts all the time. At Martha's Vineyard in Massachusetts, the cliffs are being worn away at a rate of about five feet a year. The lighthouse there has been moved inland three times.

✳ Hunters in the Western world pride themselves on the efficiency of their weapons, which are usually guns, and on their own ability to fire those guns accurately.

In Malaya, a group of tribal huntsmen, the Sakai, have a much more delicate—but equally accurate—weapon: the blowpipe. They take along this long, hollow rod when they roam the jungles in search of fruit and animals.

When they sight a creature in a treetop, they blow into the barrel, and a thin dart flies out and kills the prey. To ensure its effectiveness, the tip of the dart is dipped in a poisonous substance before it is inserted into the blowpipe.

❋ If you looked out of your train window in Llanfair, Wales, you would see a strange sign. It is actually one long sign above the platform, and it has this on it:

**LLANFAIRPWLLGWYNGYLL-
GOGERYCHWYRNDROBWLL-
LLANTYSILIOGOGOGOCH**

It identifies the place in Welsh, and means: "St. Mary's church in the hollow of the white hazel near a rapid whirlpool and the church of St. Tysilio of the red cave."

❊ It's so hot in India that a great deal of the trade and business in the villages is done out in the open. Even barbers give haircuts right out in the street!

❊ Salt, at one time, was so precious a commodity that explorers set out in search of it, wars were fought over it, and some lucky people were paid for their labor in salt. That, by the way, is how we got the world *salary*.

So a salt mine was a treasure house. And in Hallein, in the Salzburg province of Austria, there are mountains where they have been mining for salt for more than 2,000 years. Today, the equipment is modern, but they are still going down into those mines for the same product—salt!

✳ Guilty or not guilty is the choice of a verdict for criminal offenses in all countries—except Scotland. In trials for criminal offenses there, three verdicts are permitted: guilty, not guilty—and not proven. Not proven amounts to acquittal.

✳ One of the most clever tasks of design and engineering was accomplished by Filippo Brunelleschi, an Italian architect who lived in the fifteenth century.

When he constructed the dome on the Cathedral of Florence, this Renaissance architect left a small opening in the top through which a shaft of light streams in every June 21. The opening, in its relation to the sun, was so precisely arranged that the sunbeam shines squarely on a brass plate set in the floor of the sanctuary. For more than five centuries, this ray of light has never failed to cover the plate completely.

Brunelleschi knew that once there was the slightest divergence of light from the plate it would mean that the cathedral had shifted its center of gravity and the structure would have to be bolstered to prevent its collapse. The cathedral, however, was so perfectly designed that it has stood firmly on marshy ground for nearly 600 years.

✲ It doesn't take a great invention to make money for the inventor. Many people who thought of simple little things have made fortunes from them. Here are a few examples: the man who thought of putting the rubber eraser on lead pencils made $100,000 a year; a man named Harvey Kennedy made $2.5 million for inventing the shoelace; the woman who invented a certain kind of curling iron got a yearly royalty of $40,000; and Dr. Plimpton, the inventor of the roller skate, made $1,000,000 from his patent.

✳ How short can the name of a place be? It can have just one letter! In France there is a village named Y, and A is the name of a village in Norway!

✳ Mexico City is built on an underground reservoir. Each year, the number of people in the city grows, and more water is taken out of the reservoir. As a result, the city is slowly sinking at a rate of about 6 to 8 inches a year.

❋ If you've eaten in a Chinese restaurant recently, you've probably received a fortune cookie along with the check. (By the way, fortune cookies are as American as apple pie.) The D & E Research Institute in Ithaca, New York, evaluated the effectiveness of the fortunes in these cookies.

The institute contacted the owners of local Chinese restaurants, who agreed to help with this three-week study. After restaurant guests were given their checks, had divided up their cookies, and had read their fortunes, the waitperson would record their names, addresses and phone numbers, and the fortune that was written on the message tucked in the cookie. A year later these people were contacted and asked: *In the last year, was the following statement [their fortune] true about your life?*

Amazingly, 80 percent said that the fortune predicted had come true.

Index

If you liked this book, you'll love all this series:

Little Giant® Book of "True" Ghost Stories • Little Giant® Book of "True" Ghostly Tales • Little Giant® Book of After School Fun • Little Giant® Book of Amazing Mazes • Little Giant® Book of Animal Facts • Little Giant® Book of Basketball • Little Giant® Book of Brain Twisters • Little Giant® Book of Card Games • Little Giant® Book of Card Tricks • Little Giant® Book of Cool Optical Illusions • Little Giant® Book of Dinosaurs • Little Giant® Book of Dominoes • Little Giant® Book of Eerie Thrills & Unspeakable Chills • Little Giant® Book of Giggles • Little Giant® Book of Insults & Putdowns • Little Giant® Book of Jokes • Little Giant® Book of Kids' Games • Little Giant® Book of Knock-Knocks • Little Giant® Book of Laughs • Little Giant® Book of Magic Tricks • Little Giant® Book of Math Puzzles • Little Giant® Book of Mini-Mysteries • Little Giant® Book of Optical Illusion Fun • Little Giant® Book of Optical Illusions • Little Giant® Book of Optical Tricks • Little Giant® Book of Riddles • Little Giant® Book of School Jokes • Little Giant® Book of Science Experiments • Little Giant® Book of Science Facts • Little Giant® Book of Side-Splitters • Little Giant® Book of Tongue Twisters • Little Giant® Book of Travel Fun • Little Giant® Book of Travel Games • Little Giant® Book of Tricks & Pranks • Little Giant® Book of Visual Tricks • Little Giant® Book of Weird & Wacky Facts • Little Giant® Book of Whodunits

Available at fine stores everywhere.